Edited by
P. Brett Hammond, Jr.
TIAA-CREF

Martin L. Leibowitz
Morgan Stanley

Laurence B. Siegel
Research Foundation of CFA Institute
Ounavarra Capital LLC

Rethinking the Equity Risk Premium

RESEARCH FOUNDATION
OF CFA INSTITUTE

Statement of Purpose

The Research Foundation of CFA Institute is a not-for-profit organization established to promote the development and dissemination of relevant research for investment practitioners worldwide.

The Research Foundation of CFA Institute and the Research Foundation logo are trademarks owned by The Research Foundation of CFA Institute. CFA®, Chartered Financial Analyst®, AIMR-PPS®, and GIPS® are just a few of the trademarks owned by CFA Institute. To view a list of CFA Institute trademarks and the Guide for the Use of CFA Institute Marks, please visit our website at www.cfainstitute.org.

©2011 The Research Foundation of CFA Institute

This publication is designed to provide accurate and authoritative information in regard to the subject matter covered. It is sold with the understanding that the publisher is not engaged in rendering legal, accounting, or other professional service. If legal advice or other expert assistance is required, the services of a competent professional should be sought.

ISBN 978-1-934667-44-6

23 December 2011

Editorial Staff

Maryann Dupes
Book Editor

Mary-Kate Hines
Assistant Editor

Christina Hampton
Publishing Technology Specialist

Cindy Maisannes
Manager, Publications Production

Lois Carrier
Production Specialist

Contents

CFA Institute
CE Qualified Activity
  This publication qualifies for 5 CE credits under the guidelines of
the CFA Institute Continuing Education Program.

Rethinking the Equity Risk Premium: An Overview and Some New Ideas

P. Brett Hammond, Jr.
Managing Director and Chief Investment Strategist
TIAA-CREF

Martin L. Leibowitz
Managing Director, Research
Morgan Stanley

Many investors regard the past decade as an unusual one for market returns. This view is no doubt based on their having experienced a sea change in equity market behavior, including much-lower-than-average returns, much higher volatility, two of the biggest bubbles (and their subsequent bursting) in stock market history, and rising correlations—cross-asset, cross-country, cross-sector, and intra-sector. Any longtime investment market participant will have encountered more extreme trends and events in the past 10 years than during any other 10-year period in the past seven decades.

One of the key features of this turbulent period is renewed uncertainty about what may be the most important measure in all of finance—namely, the equity risk premium, or the expected return for equities in excess of a risk-free rate:

$$ERP = E(re) - E(rf).$$

The equity risk premium, or ERP, plays a critical role for any investor in that it affects savings and spending behavior as well as the all-important allocation decision between riskless and risky assets. In that sense, it is an equilibrium concept that looks beyond any given period's specific circumstances to develop a fundamental, long-term estimate of return trends.

It should be noted that the equity risk premium, as the term is used here, is not identical to the historical excess return. For example, for the 10 years beginning in the middle of 2001, annualized geometric mean U.S. equity returns significantly trailed U.S. TIPS (Treasury Inflation-Protected Securities)—roughly 3 percent versus 6 percent. So, one measure of the historical excess return is −3 percent.[1] In this volume, Robert Arnott shows that, using rolling 20-year returns, the historical excess return has ranged from +20 percent to −10 percent,

---

[1]Please note that, by convention, the return is often expressed as a "percentage" rather than "percentage points."

a range that is not very helpful in forming a historical average. But these numbers do not say much about the equity risk premium, which is a forward-looking expectations-driven estimate of stock returns. In other words, what premium do we *expect* stocks to provide over a risk-free rate? This forward-looking premium is critical to fundamental activities in investing, especially strategic and tactical asset allocation but also in portfolio management, hedging, investment product development, and the formation of saving and spending plans.

The problem posed by recent history for all these activities is whether we can be confident in our understanding of equity risk. After several decades during which realized equity returns followed a welcome positive pattern, the past decade has seen a marked downturn in equities. This downturn has prompted some investors to suggest that we must permanently adjust our future expectations for equity returns versus other broad asset classes. Others argue that the same evidence suggests equities are poised for outstanding future excess returns. Which is it?

To investigate the ERP in more depth, we could evaluate forecasts, trends, and expected variations in forward-looking measures: P/Es, dividend payouts, debt, macroeconomic growth and inflation, investment horizon, demographic change, and other variables. We have at our disposal, arguably, more analytical techniques and sources of information than ever before that bear on asset class expectations and behavior, but we have less certainty than ever about the ERP.

This volume is the result of an effort to sort through and present some of the best recent thinking on the ERP in a way that practitioners may find useful in developing their own approach to the subject. It assembles leading practitioners and academics who have confronted the question of what the ERP might be going forward and, more importantly, what factors are the most important drivers of the premium.

Initial ERP Project

The present project arose out of an interest on the part of the Research Foundation of CFA Institute to revisit, in light of what has happened in asset markets, a similar but not identical effort that it sponsored in late 2001. This earlier effort emerged as the "dot-com" bubble burst and investors confronted, for the first time in many years, the possibility of an extended period of lower equity returns. The 2001 forum gathered a wide range of experts to discuss the theoretical foundations of the ERP, historical results, then-current estimates of the size of the premium, and implications for asset management (Association for Investment Management and Research 2002). It featured lively discussions of the definition of the ERP, rational expectations versus behavioral explanations for its existence, specific factors and models that explain its size and stability (or lack thereof), the possibility of structural change–driven effects on the premium, and ways in which institutions and individuals incorporate views on the ERP into asset allocation.

Rather than a firm consensus, a strong sense of diversity arose from this earlier forum regarding views on the ERP and possible explanations for differences among those views. For example, **Exhibit 1** shows, as of 2001, a selected set of estimates of the ERP ranging from 0 to 7 percent, with an average of a little less than 4 percent.

Exhibit 1. Estimates as of 2001 of the ERP

Source	ERP Estimate (%)
Arnott and Bernstein (2002)	0.0
Campbell and Shiller (2001)	0.0
McGrattan and Prescott (2001)	0.0
Ross, Goetzmann, and Brown (1995)	Low
Reichenstein (2001)	1.3
Campbell (2001)	1.5–2.5
Philips (2003)	1.0–3.0
Siegel (2002)	2.0
Bansal and Lundblad (2002)	2.5
Shoven (2001)	3.0
Siegel (1994)	3.0–4.0
Asness (2000)	4.0
Graham and Harvey (2001)	4.0
Ibbotson and Chen (2003)	4.0
Goyal and Welch (2002)	3–5
Fama and French (2002)	4.3
Cornell (1999)	5.0
Ibbotson and Sinquefield (1976)	5.0
Welch (2000)	6.0–7.0
Average	3.7
Range	0.0–7.0

Note: ERP estimates are the expected long-term geometric return of equities in excess of the real risk-free rate.

Figure 1 summarizes, in schematic form, some of the key dimensions that can help explain these estimates. On one dimension, differences in ERP estimates can be caused by the weight given to short-term versus long-term investment horizons, including an emphasis on mean reversion or cyclicality. (A related dimension, not shown here, for different regimes or macro environments could

Figure 1. Three-Dimensional Array of Views on the ERP

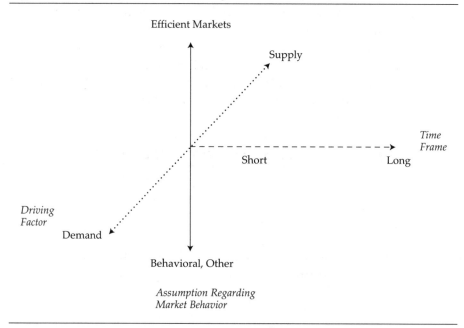

also be added—for example, whether prevailing interest rates are high or low.) ERP estimates can also vary according to whether supply or demand considerations are the dominant influence. Some investigators focus on the demand for a return that will compensate investors for the extra risk of equities, whereas others look at the supply of cash flows that companies can inject into the market.

Perhaps most fundamentally, the forum exposed different views on investor behavior, specifically whether markets exhibit rational expectations or suffer from behavioral distortions, such as myopic loss aversion (which can be non-linear or noncontinuous). One area of general agreement was that, to their detriment, few institutions or individuals explicitly address these issues and even fail to consider the size of the equity premium itself in forming policy portfolios and determining asset allocation.

10th Anniversary Project

The current project started with leading academics and practitioners gathering for a daylong discussion on what new developments, if any, have occurred in thinking about the ERP as well as in estimating the size of the ERP that we can expect in the future. Following that discussion, participants were asked to set down their current thoughts in essay form. The result, contained in this volume, is a rich set of papers that illuminate the issues and speak to the conceptual and empirical sources of the various perspectives. What is interesting about the more recent effort is not only some commonality with respect to the emphasis on supply-driven considerations but also—quite naturally in light of recent history and theory—a great deal of variation among the authors on the stability and term structure of the ERP as well as on whether variations in the ERP, no matter what their source, matter much.

The opening paper by Roger Ibbotson lays out several ways of estimating the ERP, including supply, demand, historical extrapolation, and combinations thereof. Investors are not the only agents who are affected by the excess return on equities over bonds; corporations should consider the ERP as the most important ingredient in understanding their cost of capital, and equity analysts need to use the ERP as part of the discount rate when estimating the present value of a company's future cash flows. Moreover, although it may be the largest market premium, the ERP is not the only one. Other premiums are associated with investment horizon, company size, value, momentum, default risk, and inflation risk. Of particular interest is the liquidity premium, described by Ibbotson as the phenomenon in which unpopular stocks (those that do not trade much) can display significant excess returns compared with stocks traded more often. Most important, investors often fail to differentiate a short-term tactical view of the ERP from the more fundamental long-term supply-driven equilibrium equity premium, suggesting that short-term signals may not always provide accurate information about the "true" long-term ERP.

Focusing on the cyclical nature of returns and fundamental indicators, Clifford Asness notes that there is no evidence that high P/Es are an accurate forecast of high future earnings growth rates. Rather, the evidence runs in the opposite direction. Using his own estimates of earnings growth and drawing on the Shiller P/E, which is the current price divided by trailing 10-year average real earnings, Asness offers a future equity return estimate in the range of 4 percent. Because it is hard to agree on a benchmark for the risk-free rate, he does not make a specific forecast of the ERP.

Looking historically and adopting a broad geographical perspective, Elroy Dimson, Paul Marsh, and Mike Staunton report on their most recent update of realized excess equity returns, relative to both bills and bonds, in 19 different countries from 1900 to the start of 2011. Although they found considerable variation across countries, the realized excess return was substantial everywhere. For their world index, annualized geometric mean real returns were 5.5 percent, the excess return relative to Treasury bills was 4.5 percent, and the excess return relative to long-term government bonds was 3.8 percent. Based on a supply model of the ERP, with the addition of the change in the real exchange rate, they estimate that the forward-looking equity premium is lower, around 3–3.5 percent, largely because of lower expected dividend growth compared with the historical average. In addition, they suggest that mean reversion in the stock market may not be as strong a force as others would argue. And even if mean reversion is a force, it may not provide much comfort to an investor who still does not know what the average stock market return will be in the future, nor what the equity premium is today or what the other parameters of the return process are.

The paper by Richard Grinold, Kenneth Kroner, and Laurence Siegel develops and estimates a supply model of the ERP. It decomposes equity returns into three major components: income, earnings growth, and repricing:

$$R \underbrace{\frac{D}{P} - \Delta S}_{\text{Income}} + \underbrace{i + g}_{\text{Earnings growth}} + \underbrace{\Delta \text{PE}}_{\text{Repricing}},$$

where D/P is the dividend yield, ΔS is share repurchases net of (that is, minus) new issuance, i is inflation, g is real earnings growth (not earnings per share), and the last term is the change in the P/E multiple. To illustrate, if the current 10-year bond yield is 2 percent and the ERP is 4 percent, then income, earnings growth, and repricing components must sum to 6 percent. Looking forward, the authors estimate future income to be about 2 percent, composed of dividend yield of about 1.8 percent and net share repurchases at 0.2 percent (repurchases of 2.2 percent and dilution or new issues at 2 percent). Earnings growth is expected to be a little more than 5 percent, with 2.4 percent coming from inflation and a little less than 3 percent coming from real earnings growth (which they equate to real GDP growth). Finally, although repricing contributed significantly to equity returns in the 20th century, there is little reason to believe that it will continue to do so. If we put these figures together, equity returns are expected to be about 7.2 percent. If the long-term nominal bond yield is about 3 percent, then the ERP is in the range of 4 percent.

Robert Arnott supports a view of the ERP as cyclical, smaller, and more dynamic than the prevailing theory of a more stable and robust premium would suggest. He counters a series of "myths" by showing that bonds have outperformed stocks over a significant period, the realized excess return has often been lower than the forward-looking ERP, net stock buybacks are lower than is often assumed, lower earnings yields are empirically associated with lower subsequent stock returns and premiums, real earnings and stock prices grow with per capita GDP rather than total GDP, and dividend yields are lower now than ever before. When taking this more sobering evidence into account, he finds that the probability of future stock returns matching the 7 percent real historical average is slight. Arnott's estimate of the future ERP ranges from negative to slightly positive.

Antti Ilmanen directly addresses the issue of the stability of the ERP over time by considering what the premium might look like for the next decade and well beyond, including periods with regime and term structure variations. After helpfully reviewing a wide variety of approaches to the ERP, he makes three major points. First, term structure effects are more obvious on the bond side of the premium, where short-dated TIPS yields are currently negative but longer-dated TIPS are higher, implying a 2.7 percent forward TIPS yield for the decade starting in 2021. Second, abnormally high (or low) starting valuations for equity markets and related mean-reversion potential have strong implications for expected stock market returns for the next few years. However, if we consider prospective equity returns *after* the next decade, we have no clue what the starting valuation levels will be in 2021. Thus, if we assume below-average equity market returns for the next decade because of an expected normalization of the currently high Shiller P/E, our best forecast for real equity market returns beyond 2021 should be closer to our "unconditional" long-term return forecasts. That is, these forward forecasts should largely ignore starting valuations (or at least allow future higher starting yields in 2021 than in 2011). And third, many indicators besides valuation measures can be used to predict stock market returns. Regressions and other econometric techniques can be used to forecast returns over any investment horizon (admittedly having fewer independent data points in longer horizon regressions). It is thus possible to estimate a full term structure of expected returns.

Using a variation on the supply-driven approach, Peng Chen looks at whether bonds might outperform stocks over the long run as they have over the past decade. Although the bulk of bond returns comes from their yield or income, the recent outperformance of bonds is based on the decline in yield (price increase). Currently, long-term bond yields are so low (estimated at the time of writing to be less than 3 percent) that they are unlikely to decline much further, so expected capital gains from bonds are low to negative. In contrast, stock returns depend on earnings growth and the change in the ratio of price to earnings as well as their yield. If expected earnings growth and yields remain at roughly historical averages (5 percent and 2 percent, respectively), then P/Es have to decline to 5 to produce overall future stock returns less than the 4 percent expected bond yield—an outcome that seems highly unlikely.

Looking at the information contained in the P/E that might bear on the ERP, Andrew Ang and Xiaoyan Zhang conclude that the ERP is relatively stable over time. They decompose companies' future earnings into those associated with a perpetual, no-growth component and a component associated with future growth opportunities. In effect, movements in P/E reflect changes in discount rates, which contain the ERP, as well as growth opportunities, which involve the cash flow and earnings-generating capacity of company investments. Therefore, P/Es can be high (low) because growth opportunities are favorable and/or because expected returns are low. Using more than 50 years of data from the S&P 500 Index, Ang and Zhang show that macro variables—especially risk-free rates, earnings growth, and payout ratios—are important in explaining variations in P/E. Most important, although discount rates (which contain the ERP) are variable, they are also mean reverting; thus, changes in growth opportunities, rather than in the total discount rate, explain 95 percent of the variation in P/E.

Adopting a historical emphasis, as several of the other authors have, Jeremy Siegel looks back even further to emphasize continuities in the numbers that underlie the historical excess return and estimates of the ERP. He shows that the underperformance of real equity returns in the past 10 years relative to the historical average (6–7 percent) was just about offset by the outperformance of the previous 10 years. In addition, the average historical P/Es and earnings yields have changed very little in the past decade, further supporting the notion of stability in the forward-looking ERP. Siegel closes by observing, consistent with finance theory, that the dividend payout ratio has declined along with dividend yield but that it was offset by the growth of future earnings and dividends.

Rajnish Mehra looks back in a different way, asking whether the result of his original groundbreaking work, which predicted a very low ERP, is still warranted. Taking a long-term view that combines supply and demand considerations, he argues that higher estimates of the ERP typically depend on three basic assumptions that need rethinking because they lead to overestimations of aggregate risk. First, the risk-free rate of return should be matched to the duration of liabilities, which suggests using higher inflation-linked bond or mortgage returns rather than the more commonly used T-bill rate. Second, most estimates ignore the idea that households borrow considerably more than they lend, thus inflating the ERP. Third, younger investors have a higher demand for equities than middle-aged and older investors, but younger investors find it harder than older investors to borrow. These life-cycle and borrowing constraints artificially raise the ERP and the bond yield. Taken together, these corrections greatly reduce forward ERP estimates. One consequence of this analysis is that as the Baby Boomers retire and raise the demand for bonds, it is possible that the ERP will be higher in the future.

In sum, the papers collected in this volume share a general emphasis on supply factors and models for the historical excess return as well as the forward-looking equity risk premium. After 10 years of low and highly volatile equity returns, there is little consensus about the stability of the ERP over changing regimes and time horizons. Interestingly, the group appears to be in agreement more on the actual size of the ERP over the next few years (most agree that it is in the 4 percent range) than on its stability.

Another Perspective: Regimes and Circumstantial Drivers

Rather than try to resolve what may be unresolvable differences in perspective on the ERP, and given the understandable challenges of evidence, inference, and prediction in this area, it may be useful to adopt a different approach—one that acknowledges and reflects the inherent multiplicity and diversity among (1) interest rate and market regimes and (2) investor perspectives.

The ERP is typically discussed as an expected return increment needed to compensate a universal or typical investor for accepting equity risk. This simple, and thus attractive, definition tempts us to think of a single investor deciding, on the margin, whether to move from a "riskless" fixed-income base into equities. The higher the ERP, the more the investor can expect to gain from a move from fixed income to equities and the higher the expected allocation to stocks. The lower the risk premium, the lower the expected gain and the lower the allocation to equities.

One implication of this single-premium concept is the assumption that it is possible to forecast a single "headline" ERP. This assumption is built into most discussions of the risk premium and most applications. Of course, these discussions and applications must take into account variables that affect the headline number. **Exhibit 2** is a far-from-exhaustive list of these "objective" drivers, including the selection of the risk-free asset base, the type of equities under consideration, real interest rate regimes, inflation expectations, other macro trends, earnings expectations, variations in the premium over time, and other considerations that can affect the forecast of a risk premium.

Each of these important variables can drive differences in calculations of the ERP. These variables have received considerable attention from analysts as well as from academics in search of the actual risk premium, including many of the contributors to this volume. Some of the differences in perspectives may be better understood by noting that the dynamics among macroeconomic and valuation factors, and their effects on the ERP, may be nonlinear. This nonlinearity can be seen in an admittedly simplistic form in **Exhibit 3**, in which the analysis is tied to interest rate regimes, which are nonlinearly associated with equity valuations. In other words, one can observe a sweet spot in P/Es and other valuations associated with moderate real long-term interest rates (2–3 percent), with a drop in valuations for lower and higher interest rate regimes. The relationships among some of the factors listed here display loosely connected tendencies rather than strong tight unities (e.g., inflation).

Exhibit 2. Objective Drivers of ERP Differences

Risk-Free Asset	Equity Class	Real Interest Rate Trend	Inflation Expectations	Other Macro Assumptions	Earnings Expectations	Dividend Trend	ERP Variations
Treasury bills	U.S. equities	High	High	Macroeconomy	High	Rising	Volatility
Treasury notes	Global equities	Medium	Medium	Demographics	Medium	Falling	Volatility of volatility
Inflation-linked bonds	Large cap	Low	Low	Globalization	Low		
	Other:						
	Size						
	Value						
	Geography						
	Sector						

Exhibit 3.   Real Interest Rate Regimes and the ERP

Factor	Low Rates 0–1%	Sweet Spot 2–3%	High Rates 6%+
Equity risk premium	High (6%)	Low (4% or less)	High (5%)
Probability of occurrence	Low	High	Low
Financial/economic environment	Dismal	Balanced	Overheated
Inflation expectations	Low (1–2%)	Low/medium (2–3%)	High (4%+)
Discount rate/cost of capital	Medium (7%)	Medium (7%)	High (11%)
Real growth rate	Very low (2.5%)	Good (4%)	Too high (7%)
Regime persistence	Hopefully brief	Sustainable	Almost surely brief
Sustainability of current earnings	Fair (0.4)	Fair (0.4)	Good (0.7)
New investment profitability	Good when available (6%)	Good (6%)	Squeezed (2%)
"Franchise" value (FV)	Low (4.8)	High (11.4)	Low (3.2)
"Ongoing" or "tangible" value (TV)	Fair (5.7)	Fair (5.7)	Fair (6.4)
Theoretical P/E (FV + TV)	Low (10.5)	Peak (17.1)	Low (9.6)

Notes: Specific functional values have no empirical validity. They are illustrative of relative values that might be associated with P/E and other valuation components corresponding to the three growth regimes.
Source: Based on Leibowitz and Bova (2007).

The main point is the relationship between the ERP and other economic and valuation factors. Note that although the middle, or medium, interest rate regime is the sweet spot for the economy and the equity market, the ERP could remain low in these circumstances. Whether we focus on supply or demand forces, excess return expectations may be low compared with those in more uncertain times when economies are troubled or overheated. So, some of the differences in views of the ERP could be attributed to specific regime forecasts or to whether regimes play a strong or weak role in determining the ERP.

One implication of looking at these sorts of objective determinants is that they are all, at least in theory, reducible. In other words, let's imagine it is possible to gather investors together to obtain a general agreement on selection of the risk-free asset, equity index, earnings and inflation expectations, and even the pattern by which the ERP varies over time or the list of forces that cause such variation. Although agreement on these matters might not be easy to obtain, discussions would focus on issues that are subject to measurement, analysis, and objective inference. With such a general agreement, some or maybe even a great portion of the differences among investors in their ERP estimates would be reduced. But not completely.

The differences in investors' ERP estimates would not, in the end, be eliminated. These differences are not fully reducible even with agreement on measurement and benchmarks. What remains are irreducible differences based on investors' varying conditions or circumstances. Each investor might have a unique combination of circumstances that differentiates her from all other investors, not in terms of her views on how to calculate the ERP but in terms of the circumstances in which she finds herself as an investor. In turn, those unique circumstances can then affect what we might call a "personal" or "institutional" ERP, one that is specific to an individual or institution. As shown in **Exhibit 4**, these circumstances could include investment horizon, need for liquidity, rebalancing requirement, sensitivity to changing market valuations, the capacity to evaluate those changing valuations, risk tolerance, and buyer or seller orientation.

All these circumstantial drivers of investor perceptions can affect the size of the equity premium that an investor might expect or experience at any point in time. Furthermore, this expected ERP is different from a "required" ERP in that it reflects what the investor actually experiences based on his or her individual circumstances (as opposed to an ERP that is required for the investor to act). For example, investment horizon can range from nearly perpetual (some foundations and endowments) to nearly immediate (an individual investor's current living expenses). A short-term investor might not experience the same ERP as a long-term investor, either in terms of expected return or expected volatility of that return. Similarly, liquidity needs can affect the return an investor can expect; sometimes there may be a positive or negative illiquidity premium built into the ERP. And rebalancing requirements can influence return, especially if we are aware that a large set of investors must rebalance in the same direction at the same time. In turn, the ERP may vary depending on whether one is a buyer or seller (such as during late 2008 in the equity markets, when bid–ask spreads or the differential returns required by buyers and sellers froze some markets and nearly destroyed others).

Take, for example, some combinations of these dimensions as illustrated in Exhibit 4. Many long-term investors are relatively premium insensitive in that they are interested in holding rather than buying or selling. Others, such as the LSB (long-horizon valuation-sensitive buyer), may be looking to add to positions if the price (premium) is right, although the LSS (long-horizon valuation-sensitive seller) is looking to lighten holdings based on receiving an adequate premium.[2] In contrast, a liquidity-sensitive investor (e.g., hedge funds in mid-2007 and late 2008), denoted by LLS, may need to sell at nearly any

---

[2]See the notes to Exhibit 4 for a full explanation of the acronyms used in this discussion.

Exhibit 4. Circumstantial Drivers of Investors' Perceptions of the ERP

Investor Type	Investment Horizon	Liquidity Bias	Rebalancing Requirement	Valuation Sensitivity	Ability to Evaluate Market	Risk Tolerance	Trade Orientation	Example
Long horizon								
LSB	Long			Sensitive	High		Buyer	Discretionary buyer looking for low premium
LSS	Long			Sensitive	Low		Seller	Discretionary seller looking for extra premium
LLB	Long	Liquidity bias					Buyer	Buyer at nearly any price
LLS	Long	Liquidity bias					Seller	Seller at nearly any price
LRB or LRS	Long		Rebalance				Buyer	Must rebalance when market moves
LCB or LCS	Long				High	Constant		Constant risk tolerance but evaluates and acts on changing market opportunities
LVB or LVS	Long				High	Variable		Risk tolerance depends on market conditions or changing personal circumstances
LRB or LRS	Long					Range bound		Constant risk tolerance, except in extreme market move
Short horizon								
SSB or SSS	Short			Sensitive				Daily, weekly, monthly, quarterly performance evaluation
SLB or SLS	Short	Liquidity bias						Must remain liquid

Notes: First letter: L = long horizon, S = short horizon. Second letter: S = valuation sensitive, L = liquidity bias, C = constant risk tolerance, V = variable risk tolerance, R = has rebalancing requirement. Third letter: B = buyer, S = seller.

price in order to raise cash. Other investors, such as pension funds, may need to put cash to work quickly as contributions come in the door (LLB). Still others may need to rebalance systematically as the market pushes their allocations away from a policy portfolio (LRB or LRS), and therefore, they may be relatively premium insensitive. Of course, the same individual or institution may exhibit more than one of these behaviors depending on the circumstances. The point is that these circumstances can influence the size and character of the ERP investors experience or require.

Shorter-term investors may be a smaller part of the overall equity market but may receive an outsize portion of media attention. If we put aside share repurchases and new issues, as well as the supply of equity substitutes, the term structure of the ERP and its volatility may be such that both variables have very different values over the short and long term. A high short-term volatility may look much more acceptable to a long-term investor because of his ability to ride it out. Similarly, a high short-term premium can coexist with a dreary long-term premium.

So, long-term and short-term investors might share a sensitivity to valuation metrics but in very different ways. Long-term valuation-sensitive investors (LSB and LSS) might respond to a sufficiently high long-term ERP (that is, the ERP in excess of the long-term fixed-income yield) by selling bonds to buy stocks in the belief that such an action will compensate them for long-term nominal as well as real risk. In contrast, short-term valuation-sensitive investors (SSB and SSS) may be more inclined to judge the ERP either on an absolute stand-alone basis or relative to returns from various fixed-income durations given expectations regarding yield curve movements. In these cases, price volatility looms large as a risk factor, so short-term investors need a much greater premium inducement to get them to prefer equities to bonds over their short horizon.

One should also consider not just the effects of circumstantial ERP on investor behavior but also the effects of investor behavior on the ERP. As buyers and sellers meet in the marketplace, the transaction size, urgency, other asset holdings, and other circumstances could dampen or exacerbate equity premium movements. Rebalancers and especially liquidity-sensitive sellers may be relatively insensitive to price and premium and thus have a moderating effect on ERP variations. Both valuation-sensitive and valuation-insensitive investors could affect the equity premium. Valuation-sensitive investors are looking for a desired or required price or premium, so their actions will tend to move the market in that direction. The impact of actions by valuation-insensitive investors may be unpredictable because they purchase or sell shares at times that could inadvertently push the equity premium up or down.

Some transactions, however, might have little effect on the marginal ERP. In general, the marginal ERP value is likely to be determined by one type of buyer interacting with one type of seller. Although we often think of both the marginal buyer and seller as savvy and valuation sensitive, an equally savvy investor on one side may not be able to exercise valuation sensitivity. For example, a long-term liquidity-sensitive buyer (LLB) might be content buying at a price set by a short-term valuation-sensitive seller (SSS) who thinks that equities are currently overpriced. The sum of all such forces would theoretically combine into a pair of supply and demand curves, which could be smooth, lumpy, kinked, and certainly multidimensional (e.g., with term structure characteristics and regime dependency). Thus, we can see how the interplay of these multiple circumstantial forces can lead to a risk premium that is far more multifaceted and complex than is typically envisioned in the standard discount models, even when we take into account structural and cyclical changes in the more objective factors cited in Exhibit 2.

Overlaid on all these issues may be behavioral effects, such as systematic investor misperceptions and behavioral anomalies, that affect buying and selling behavior (the behavioral versus efficient markets dimension in Figure 1). But these forces are in addition to the objective and circumstantial forces just described, and they may be more invariant. Finally, our investor categories are not all mutually exclusive, and depending on circumstances, investors may shift from one type to another.

Conclusion

The past 10 years have shown that the ERP, far from being a settled matter, continues to challenge analysts. The research and observations in this volume have a number of implications for investment practice and theory. First, investors and analysts should take care to be explicit about their estimates of the ERP. We still too often use different definitions of, assumptions about, and approaches to the ERP, or leave it altogether implicit in our analyses of asset markets and valuations. Further clarity may help reduce the number of occasions when we are talking past each other. Second, we should be clear about what model we are using when we offer a forecast or explanation of the ERP. We have seen that variations in our estimates can be the result of different approaches to objective, circumstantial, and behavioral factors. Third, differing circumstances among investors lead to true, irreducible differences in the ERP that each investor may face at any given time. This final consideration underscores how the interplay of these multiple circumstantial forces can lead to a risk premium that is far more multifaceted and complex than typically envisioned in the standard discount models, even when we take into account structural and cyclical changes in the more objective factors. The papers contained in this volume richly illustrate this interplay.

References

Arnott, Robert D., and Peter L. Bernstein. 2002. "What Risk Premium Is 'Normal'?" *Financial Analysts Journal*, vol. 58, no. 2 (March/April):64–85.

Asness, Clifford S. 2000. "Stocks versus Bonds: Explaining the Equity Risk Premium." *Financial Analysts Journal*, vol. 56, no. 2 (March/April):96–113.

Association for Investment Management and Research. 2002. *Equity Risk Premium Forum.* Charlottesville, VA: Association for Investment Management and Research (www.cfapubs.org/toc/cp.1/2002/2002/7).

Bansal, Ravi, and Christian Lundblad. 2002. "Market Efficiency, Asset Returns, and the Size of the Risk Premium in Global Equity Markets." *Journal of Econometrics*, vol. 109, no. 2 (August):195–237.

Campbell, John Y. 2001. "Forecasting U.S. Equity Returns in the 21st Century." In *Estimating the Real Rate of Return on Stocks Over the Long Term*. Washington, DC: Social Security Advisory Board (August).

Campbell, John Y., and Robert J. Shiller. 2001. "Valuation Ratios and the Long-Run Stock Market Outlook: An Update." NBER Working Paper 8221 (April).

Cornell, Bradford. 1999. *The Equity Risk Premium: The Long-Run Future of the Stock Market.* New York: John Wiley & Sons.

Fama, Eugene F., and Kenneth R. French. 2002. "The Equity Premium." *Journal of Finance*, vol. 57, no. 2 (April):637–659.

Goyal, Amit, and Ivo Welch. 2002. "Predicting the Equity Premium with Dividend Ratios." NBER Working Paper 8788 (February).

Graham, John R., and Campbell R. Harvey. 2001. "The Theory and Practice of Corporate Finance: Evidence from the Field." *Journal of Financial Economics*, vol. 60, nos. 2–3 (May):187–243.

Ibbotson, Roger G., and Peng Chen. 2003. "Long-Run Stock Returns: Participating in the Real Economy." *Financial Analysts Journal*, vol. 59, no. 1 (January/February):88–98.

Ibbotson, Roger G., and Rex A. Sinquefield. 1976. "Stocks, Bonds, Bills, and Inflation: Year-by-Year Historical Returns (1926–1974)." *Journal of Business*, vol. 49, no. 1 (January):11–47.

Leibowitz, Martin L., and Anthony Bova. 2007. "P/Es and Pension Funding Ratios." *Financial Analysts Journal*, vol. 63, no. 1 (January/February):84–96.

McGrattan, Ellen R., and Edward C. Prescott. 2001. "Taxes, Regulations, and Asset Prices." NBER Working Paper 8623 (December).

Philips, Thomas K. 2003. "Estimating Expected Returns." *Journal of Investing*, vol. 12, no. 3 (Fall):49–57.

Reichenstein, William. 2001. "The Investment Implications of Lower Stock Return Prospects." *AAII Journal*, vol. 23, no. 9 (October):4–7.

Ross, Stephen A., William N. Goetzmann, and Stephen J. Brown. 1995. "Survival." *Journal of Finance*, vol. 50, no. 3 (July):853–873.

Shoven, John B. 2001. "What Are Reasonable Long-Run Rates of Return to Expect on Equities?" In *Estimating the Real Rate of Return on Stocks Over the Long Term*. Washington, DC: Social Security Advisory Board (August).

Siegel, Jeremy J. 1994. *Stocks for the Long Run: A Guide to Selecting Markets for Long-Term Growth*. Burr Ridge, IL: Irwin.

———. 2002. *Stocks for the Long Run: The Definitive Guide to Financial Market Returns and Long-Term Investment Strategies*. 3rd ed. New York: McGraw-Hill.

Welch, Ivo. 2000. "Views of Financial Economists on the Equity Premium and on Professional Controversies." *Journal of Business*, vol. 73, no. 4 (October):501–537.

The Equity Risk Premium

Roger G. Ibbotson

Professor in Practice, Yale School of Management
Chairman, Zebra Capital Management

The equity risk premium (ERP) is a concept that seems to mean different things to different people. Some people treat it as the equilibrium long-run return, whereas others treat it as their own personal estimate of the long-run return. Some discuss it as a future return, whereas others discuss it as a realized return. Some compare equity returns with long-term bond returns or yields, whereas others compare equity returns with short-term bond returns or yields. There are various ways to estimate the ERP, whether we are talking about equilibrium or personal estimates and whether we are making forecasts or measuring past realizations. In this paper, I will clarify the terminology, compare the various ways of estimating and measuring the equity risk premium, and discuss some of the other premiums that exist in both equity and other capital markets.

What is the equity risk premium? I consider it a long-run equilibrium concept that gives an estimate of the future excess return of the stock market over and above the bond market. There are several advantages to thinking of the ERP as an equilibrium concept. It provides the *market's* estimate of the excess return on stocks relative to bonds. It is neutral in the sense that it does not take advantage of any particular investor's expertise but, rather, tries to determine what the market thinks. In this way, it can be used as a benchmark for more active or dynamic forecasts of the stock market. It can also be used for long-term planning purposes in setting a long-term asset allocation or in estimating the returns that a portfolio can provide to meet various future obligations.

I have already established that from an investor's perspective, the ERP is the expected return that investors can earn on stocks in excess of bonds. From a corporation's perspective, however, the ERP is part of the cost of equity capital. When looking at a company's entire weighted average cost of capital, the ERP is usually the most important ingredient. From a valuation perspective, the ERP is used as part of the discount rate when estimating the present value of a set of future cash flows. The expected return of equity is used in all three of these contexts, and they are all equivalent to each other after taking into account certain market imperfections, such as taxes and transaction costs.

Methods of Estimating the Equity Risk Premium

How should we estimate the equity risk premium in equilibrium over the long run? There are four primary ways. The first is to look at the historical ERPs that we get from comparing past stock returns with past bond returns. These realizations give us an idea as to the magnitude of payoffs that investors have received for taking on the extra risk of being in the stock market rather than the various bond markets. A second way is to use a consensus estimate of the opinions of all the participants in the marketplace. Because these market participants are setting the price, they must also be the investors who are buying or selling stocks to reflect their long-term outlook. A third method is to look at the demand side of the equation. In this case, we are trying to determine how much extra return an investor would demand for taking on the extra risk of buying stocks rather than bonds. The last way is to look at the supply side of the equation. Here we consider what the economy and corporations supply to the market in the form of earnings or cash flow.

Historical. Let us start with the historical perspective. **Table 1** lists the returns over the period 1926 through 2010 for the following Ibbotson indices: Large Company Stocks, Small Company Stocks, Long-Term Corporate Bonds, Long-Term Government Bonds, Intermediate-Term Government Bonds, U.S. Treasury Bills, and Inflation. The geometric mean annualized return from Large Company Stocks was 9.9 percent, and the arithmetic mean return was 11.9 percent. The Long-Term Government Bond geometric mean return was 5.5 percent, and the arithmetic mean return was 5.9 percent. The U.S. Treasury Bill geometric mean return was 3.6 percent, and the arithmetic mean return was 3.7 percent. The table demonstrates that there can be many

Table 1. Ibbotson Index Series: Summary Statistics of Annual Total Return, 1926–2010

Series	Geometric Mean	Arithmetic Mean	Standard Deviation
Large Company Stocks	9.9%	11.9%	20.4%
Small Company Stocks	12.1	16.7	32.6
Long-Term Corporate Bonds	5.9	6.2	8.3
Long-Term Government Bonds	5.5	5.9	9.5
Intermediate-Term Government Bonds	5.4	5.5	5.7
U.S. Treasury Bills	3.6	3.7	3.1
Inflation	3.0	3.1	4.2

Source: Ibbotson® SBBI®, *2011 Classic Yearbook: Market Results for Stocks, Bonds, Bills, and Inflation, 1926–2010* (Chicago: Morningstar, 2011).

ERPs even when using a single historical data period. At the high extreme, the arithmetic mean ERP of Large Company Stocks compared with U.S. Treasury Bills was 8.2 percent (11.9 percent − 3.7 percent). At the low extreme, the geometric mean ERP of Large Company Stocks compared with Long-Term Government Bonds was 4.4 percent (9.9 percent − 5.5 percent). Thus, researchers and investors often have confusing conversations with each other. Even when they might agree on the *same* historical time interval and dataset, the ERP historical measure can be anywhere in the range of 4.4–8.2 percent, depending on which definition of ERP is used.

Investors typically use the Large Company Stock geometric mean return minus the Long-Term Government Bond return as their characterization of the historical ERP, which for 1926–2010 is 4.4 percent. In corporate finance and in valuation discounting, arithmetic means are more often used. Even if a characterization of the ERP is agreed upon, however, a debate over what historical period is most representative of the future long-run return can occur. Some might want to use even longer historical periods to reduce the estimation error, which falls in proportion to the square root of time. Some might want to use shorter and more recent periods, which better reflect the current and future environment. Those who think the historical method should be used still have plenty to debate about. The historical method, however, has the great advantage that it measures what really happened. It reveals how much stocks have actually outperformed bonds over whatever interval is under investigation.

Consensus. The consensus method might appear to be a very good approach; when using this method, one attempts to obtain the estimates from the market participants themselves (i.e., the very investors who are setting the market prices). But there are a number of problems with this approach. Most of these investors have no clear opinion about the long-run outlook. Many of them have only very short-term horizons. Individual investors often exhibit extreme optimism or pessimism and make procyclical forecasts, and so following a boom, they can have ERP estimates that exceed 20 percent or 30 percent. Following a recession or a decline in stock market prices, their estimates of the ERP might even be negative. Academics and institutional investors may be more thoughtful, but any survey of their opinions would have to be very carefully designed. I have seen surveys, however, that do not seem to even clarify whether the questionnaire refers to arithmetic mean returns or geometric mean returns. Many surveys also do not make clear whether the ERP to which they refer is the excess return of stocks over government bonds or Treasury bills or some other type of bond. This lack of clarity makes the surveys very difficult to interpret. The most extensive surveys have been done by Pablo Fernández (see, for example, Fernández, Aguirreamalloa, and Corres 2011).

Demand. The demand approach to estimating the ERP stems from the idea that investors demand an extra return for investing in stocks rather than bonds. In the capital asset pricing model (CAPM), the ERP is the central feature. The CAPM is derived from utility curves that characterize the risk–return trade-off. In the CAPM, all assets are held in the market portfolio, and the expected return of the market portfolio is sufficient to satisfy the investors' demand for stocks relative to their risk. Attempts to measure the ERP using the demand approach focus on analyzing utility functions. Mehra and Prescott (1985) first attempted to come up with reasonable measures of the ERP in this way. The ERP was very low and did not reasonably match any of the historical data. This mismatch came to be known as the "equity premium puzzle." Subsequently, many researchers have attempted to resolve the puzzle using behavioral finance, different types of utility curves, different distributional assumptions about stock returns, and risk aversion measures that are conditional on the state of the economy. In the end, the puzzle can be resolved in many ways, but the demand approach is not likely to provide a good estimate of the equity risk premium.

Supply. The supply approach attempts to estimate what the economy or the companies in the economy can supply to the market in the form of cash flows. This approach can be applied to the economy, using per capita or total GDP growth, net capital investment, and output provided to both capital and labor. It can also be applied at the corporate level, using company cash flows, earnings, dividends, payout ratios, stock share repurchases, and cash flow receipts from mergers and acquisitions. My co-authors and I used this approach in Diermeier, Ibbotson, and Siegel (1984) and in Ibbotson and Chen (2003), as did several of the authors in *The Equity Risk Premium: Essays and Explorations* (Goetzmann and Ibbotson 2006). The supply approach is a promising alternative for estimating the ERP.

Many Different Risk Premiums

Table 1 shows that the equity risk premium is not the only premium in the market. The following are some of the potential premiums:

- Long-horizon ERP (stocks – long-term government bonds)
- Short-horizon ERP (stocks – U.S. Treasury bills)
- Small-stock premium (large stocks – small stocks)
- Default premium (long-term corporate bonds – long-term government bonds)
- Horizon premium (long-term government bonds – U.S. Treasury bills)
- Real interest rate (U.S. Treasury bills – inflation)

The equity risk premium is the largest of these premiums, but all are important. We can forecast stock and bond returns of various types by restacking the various premiums. This approach is known as the "build-up method" and was first proposed in Ibbotson and Siegel (1988). **Exhibit 1** provides an example of the build-up method.

Exhibit 1. Components of Assets' Expected Returns

				Small Stocks	**Foreign Stocks**	
Stocks				Small-stock premium	Foreign stock premium	**Foreign Bonds**
Equity risk premium	**Bonds**			Equity risk premium	Equity risk premium	Foreign bond premium
Bond horizon premium	Bond horizon premium	**Cash**	**Real Estate**	Bond horizon premium	Bond horizon premium	Bond horizon premium
Real riskless rate	Real riskless rate	Real riskless rate	Real return on real estate	Real riskless rate	Real riskless rate	Real riskless rate
Inflation	Inflation	Inflation	Inflation	Inflation	Inflation	Inflation

Source: Ibbotson and Siegel (1988).

As Exhibit 1 shows, a small-stock return can be estimated from the following components: expected inflation, the expected real rate of interest, the bond horizon premium, the long-horizon ERP, and the small-stock premium. A corporate bond return can be estimated from the expected inflation rate, the expected real rate of interest, the horizon risk bond horizon premium, and the default risk premium. Often the first three terms (inflation, interest rate, and bond horizon premium) are combined into the long-term yield of a riskless bond because this yield is typically observed directly in the marketplace.

One reason that the ERP is so important is that it is often the largest number in the stack. The ERP is also the most important source of estimation error because it is not directly observable in the future. Instead, we have a historical record of past realizations and various other forecast methods. In this framework, the expected stock return is the sum of two components: the long-term riskless rate, which is the yield on bonds and is directly observable, and the long-horizon ERP, which can only be estimated.

Other Premiums in the Market

The stock market is frequently characterized by investment styles. I have discussed the small-stock premium, and investing in small- versus large-capitalization stocks is considered an investment style. Fama and French (1993), among others, proposed the other prevalent style in the marketplace. They showed that value stocks outperform growth stocks over long periods of time. They defined value stocks as those of companies that have high book-to-market ratios. Others define value stocks as having high earnings-to-price ratios (or low price-to-earnings ratios). The premiums of value over growth stocks and small over large stocks are often characterized as risk premiums because they are long term in nature, have a positive payoff, and can be earned through passive rather than active management.

Another premium in the market that has been empirically observed is the momentum premium (see, for example, Jegadeesh and Titman 1993). Stocks that did well in the previous year tend to do well in the next year, whereas stocks that did poorly in the previous year tend to do poorly again. The momentum premium is not typically characterized as an investment style because momentum investing usually involves some form of active management to realize the excess returns. There is some evidence that momentum premiums are becoming more erratic and less predictable, perhaps because momentum is becoming so well known in the market. With so many investors taking advantage of the momentum premium, it may tend to disappear over time.

The liquidity premium is perhaps as important as any of the risk premiums. Ibbotson, Diermeier, and Siegel (1984) proposed that the three security characteristics that investors most wish to avoid and, therefore, need to be most compensated for in the long run are (1) risk, (2) lack of liquidity, and (3) taxation. This observation forms part of the demand approach to expected returns because investors demand a premium to take on risk, to give up liquidity, or to invest in a security that is heavily taxed. The liquidity premium is very well known and has been applied primarily in bond and alternative asset markets. Because a bond yield is observable, a less liquid bond can easily be seen to have a higher yield than a more liquid bond that is otherwise similar. This spread is the liquidity premium, and it can be used as another stack in the build-up method described previously. Real estate and private equity are examples of alternative investments for which investors would demand a higher return in order to compensate for the fact that they cannot easily liquidate their positions. These liquidity premiums are not observable, but it is generally accepted that a substantial portion of the return that investors receive from these types of investments must be a reward for taking on this lack of liquidity.

Ibbotson, Chen, and Hu (2011) proposed a new equity investment style based on the concept of the liquidity premium. We restricted the investment universe to publicly traded stocks and found that cross-sectional differences in liquidity have a large impact on returns, even though almost every one of these stocks trades every day. Thus, the liquidity premium is important not only across asset classes but also in the continuum of liquidity within an asset class. In the case of stocks, there is a substantial difference between the returns of the most popular stocks, which are the most heavily traded, and the returns of the least popular stocks. These premiums are larger than small-stock premiums and are comparable in magnitude to value premiums. When compared with size, value, and momentum, liquidity premiums have a different but at least as powerful effect. **Table 2** provides a comparison of liquidity and size premiums.

Table 2. U.S. Equity Annual Return Quartiles, 1972–2010

	Liquidity			
Size	1 (lowest)	2	3	4 (highest)
1 (smallest)	18.17%	17.46%	13.51%	6.16%
2	16.87	15.15	11.68	6.52
3	15.15	14.36	12.87	9.56
4 (largest)	12.49	11.48	11.55	9.87

Source: Ibbotson, Chen, and Hu (2011).

Dynamic and Tactical ERP Forecasts

Most forecasts of the equity risk premium are not equilibrium forecasts. They are not attempts at estimating an ERP that can be used for long-term investment-planning purposes, the equity cost of capital in corporate finance, or the discount rate used in valuation. Rather, they are attempts to outperform the market by applying special expertise in determining whether the stock market is over- or undervalued today. Forecasts of high returns for the stock market are accompanied by recommendations to buy stocks instead of bonds, whereas low-return forecasts are accompanied by recommendations to reduce stock investments.

Of course, knowing when to buy stocks and when to sell them is very difficult, particularly at the macro level. At the individual stock level, thousands of stocks might be over- or underpriced. But at the market level, any mispricing must be systematic. For the stock market to be overpriced in aggregate, most of the individual stocks have to be overpriced, which means that the investors in aggregate must be systematically overconfident because the market price reflects their collective judgment. Most stock market forecasts implicitly say that the market is wrong in some way. The forecasters believe that their particular judgment is superior to the judgment of the marketplace.

In many cases, whether the forecaster is making an equilibrium forecast or a beat-the-market forecast is not very clear. The four approaches to the equity risk premium discussed in this paper are not always clearly classified as to whether they are being applied in an equilibrium context or for the purpose of beating the market. The historical approach is based on return realizations, but one can argue over whether they are representative of the future or are too high or low. The consensus approach is subject to incorrect measurement to such an extent that it may be difficult to apply in either context. The demand approach is usually more theoretical and is mostly useful in determining the broad direction—so that one can say that the ERP is a positive number and in equilibrium stocks should always be expected to outperform bonds in the long run. The supply approach has the most flexibility; investors can attempt to use it in an equilibrium context, or they can apply their special expertise in an attempt to outperform the market. For example, one might say that an aging population argues for lower returns in the future or that the increasing speed of technological change argues for higher returns in the future. Each expert places relative importance on a particular factor, which causes the experts to end up with a wide diversity of opinions.

Summary

I have defined what the equity risk premium is and how it can be used in equilibrium and beat-the-market contexts. The terminology is confusing to many investors and financial writers: They tend to mix up a future concept with a past realization, they assign a number to the ERP without clarifying which measurement of the ERP is being used, and they rarely clarify whether they are talking about the ERP in an equilibrium or a beat-the-market context.

I have also discussed various other premiums in the market. These premiums represent the differential returns of the many different asset classes and investment styles in the market. To make sound investment decisions, it is important to have good estimates of these premiums.

REFERENCES

Diermeier, Jeffrey J., Roger G. Ibbotson, and Laurence B. Siegel. 1984. "The Supply of Capital Market Returns." *Financial Analysts Journal*, vol. 40, no. 2 (March/April):74–80.

Fama, Eugene F., and Kenneth R. French. 1993. "Common Risk Factors in the Returns of Stocks and Bonds." *Journal of Financial Economics*, vol. 33, no. 1 (February):3–56.

Fernández, Pablo, Javier Aguirreamalloa, and Luis Corres. 2011. "Market Risk Premium Used in 56 Countries in 2011: A Survey with 6,014 Answers." Working Paper WP-920, IESE Business School (May).

Goetzmann, William N., and Roger G. Ibbotson, eds. 2006. *The Equity Risk Premium: Essays and Explorations.* New York: Oxford University Press.

Ibbotson, Roger G., and Peng Chen. 2003. "Long-Run Stock Returns: Participating in the Real Economy." *Financial Analysts Journal,* vol. 59, no. 1 (January/February):88–98.

Ibbotson, Roger G., and Laurence B. Siegel. 1988. "How to Forecast Long-Run Asset Returns." *Investment Management Review* (September/October).

Ibbotson, Roger G., Zhiwu Chen, and Wendy Y. Hu. 2011. "Liquidity as an Investment Style." Working paper, Yale University (April).

Ibbotson, Roger G., Jeffrey J. Diermeier, and Laurence B. Siegel. 1984. "The Demand for Capital Market Returns: A New Equilibrium Theory." *Financial Analysts Journal,* vol. 40, no. 1 (January/February):22–33.

Jegadeesh, Narasimhan, and Sheridan Titman. 1993. "Returns to Buying Winners and Selling Losers for Stock Market Efficiency." *Journal of Finance,* vol. 48, no. 1 (March):65–91.

Mehra, Rajnish, and Edward C. Prescott. 1985. "The Equity Premium: A Puzzle." *Journal of Monetary Economics,* vol. 15, no. 2 (March):145–161.

Reflections After the 2011 Equity Risk Premium Colloquium

Clifford Asness
Founding and Managing Principal
AQR Capital Management, LLC

In 2001, and again in 2011, I participated in a forum about the equity risk premium. Presented here are some informal thoughts about the equity premium that I composed after the second forum. These thoughts are an eclectic collection inspired by, but not limited to, what we discussed together.

Sequels Are Rarely as Good as Originals

The 2011 forum reprised the earlier gathering with many of the same presenters from 2001. When we met in 2001, it was not long after the peak of the technology bubble (I call it a bubble, although that label is still in some dispute). At that time, equity prices were still well above historical norms, although they were lower than in March 2000. In 2011, many of us would say that equity prices are still high versus historical prices, but the divergence is nowhere near as dramatic as in 2001.

We Still Do Not All Agree about Long-Term Predictability

It is clear from the 2011 forum that a division remains among the participants that was clearly present in 2001. Some believe in long-term predictability; others do not. Thus, when equity prices are high versus fundamentals (I am assuming that we agree on how to measure this comparison), some believe conditional long-term expected real equity returns are low, and vice versa.

I am in this camp, but I have to admit the relationship is not as obvious as it may seem. Point estimates—the actual observed history—show that long-term (say, 10-year) historical rolling returns are indeed negatively related to starting prices. And the market's performance since the first forum, when high prices indeed led to very low realized equity returns, might make it seem that the case is closed.

It is incredibly hard, however, to say anything with precision and confidence about the relationship between long-term return and price because not that much independent data are available and in-sample regressions often contain biases. As was mentioned in the forum, it really comes down to what an investment manager believes about long-term returns beforehand. If a manager believes that expected returns are constant, then when prices are high, expected growth will be higher than normal (making expected returns come out the same despite the higher prices). The data in fact point in the other direction, but only weakly after accounting for all the problems. In other words, the data barely help to resolve this debate.

It has to be one way or the other; it is a mathematical identity. High prices forecast either low expected returns or high expected growth. For me, despite its low statistical power, the point estimate is still a reasonable guess. Rather than looking for a definitive relationship between high prices and subsequent low returns, I find it more useful to focus on the absolute lack of evidence that high prices forecast high future growth. The relationship is equivalent, but it is how I like to frame the problem.

This point estimate is only a small part of why I believe in predictability. It is more important to me that return predictability agrees with my intuition and prior experience, largely formed from other time-series and cross-sectional experiments. A vast body of literature shows that when prices of anything are high versus fundamentals, expected returns are low, and vice versa. For instance, in the cross-section, when a given set of stocks has high prices versus fundamentals (such as book value, earnings, or cash flow), the expected returns on these stocks are low relative to other (cheaper) stocks. This finding is nearly ubiquitous. Thus, although I find the point estimate for the equity risk premium (ERP) versus the price relationship comforting, I find it far more compelling in the context of the literature. I think the way finance works is that when prices are high, as measured against any reasonable form of fundamentals, expected returns are lower than normal, and vice versa. Admittedly, that is hard to prove, especially if the focus is only on ERP data, and clearly some are still not convinced.

I posed the following question to the 2011 group, particularly to those who were skeptical about the possibility of long-term predictability: When prices are at true extremes (e.g., the high in March 2000 or the other direction, the low in the early 1980s), would forecasters project any difference in forward-looking expected real returns? If the answer is yes, the issue then is a variation in the degree of our beliefs, not a difference in dogma. (I never quite got an answer!)

Some Still Believe Silly Ideas, but They Also Have Learned Important Truths

Ten years after the technology bubble, some unsubstantiated beliefs remain. The so-called Fed model, which is the idea that high stock prices are reasonable when nominal interest rates are low, is still very common (although no one at the forum advanced this view). My own research and others' have shown this proposition to be a form of money illusion with no power to predict (even noisily) long-term stock returns. But the Fed model still yields a far more bullish forecast than focusing just on equity prices (unadjusted for nominal interest rates), as it has for a long time. Its bullishness probably accounts for its continued popularity, particularly among strategists on Wall Street.

The Shiller P/E (the current price of the S&P 500 Index divided by the previous 10-year average real earnings) has become the *lingua franca* of those that discuss the ERP and how it relates to current equity prices. This choice is not because the Shiller P/E is perfect—no measure is—but simply because it is reasonable and historically consistent. It also helps to have a common standard. Recently, the Shiller P/E has been back in the news because some broker research has called it into question. The attacks are mostly ridiculous; they are based on bullish researchers using Wall Street's long-term preferred "operating" earnings, which are earnings before negative events are deducted, or throwing out historical periods that the researchers do not want in the data. If the price of the S&P 500 is compared only with other times when the price was high, then of course it will look lower.

One argument the critics advance, with some possible merit in my view, is that the most recent financial crisis was so severe that the past 10 years of earnings are too low to be a reasonable proxy for trend. Even that effect, however, is tiny and ultimately unconvincing.[1]

Finally, reflecting the controversy about predictability discussed earlier, those who have issues with the Shiller P/E assume that today's low dividend payouts are sensible because earnings will grow more in the future. Rob Arnott and I (Arnott and Asness 2003) established empirically that this notion is not only wrong but also backward for the past 140 years. Some notions die hard, and notions that are more bullish tend to die harder. Both the Fed model and the current critique of the Shiller P/E lean in the direction of liking stocks.

More optimistically, investment managers seem to have learned some important lessons since 2001. Again, many still argue about long-term mean reversion and predictability, but many also believe, as I do, that after long-term strong returns (if mirrored in higher valuations at the end), expected future returns will be lower.

---

[1]This argument at least is in the right direction. For instance, if instead of looking at average 10-year earnings, investors looked at median 10-year earnings (thus giving no weight to the magnitude of the crisis), the resulting Shiller P/E would be very high versus history but slightly less high compared with the conventional approach of taking the average. In my view, this minor adjustment, which still shows an overvalued stock market, is not what the bulls are looking for, but it is a reasonable adjustment to make.

In contrast, in 2001, reflecting the thinking of the technology bubble, many in the investment world seemed to believe that high past returns meant *higher* long-term future returns. This belief can creep into prices in various ways, but perhaps the simplest occurs when an investor uses a past average of realized returns to forecast the future. I cannot say this view is gone, but many investors, perhaps most, now seem to understand that it never made sense.

After a time of strong long-term returns, future long-term returns will be lower. Reasonable people may believe that future long-term returns will be unaffected. No rational investor will expect long-term returns to be higher than normal; there are far fewer of such irrational investors today than in 2001.

My Forecast and Some Thoughts on Dispersion

Even those who believe in long-term predictability should acknowledge that it is a noisy process. The standard deviation of average annual returns over 10 years around a forecast that moves with the Shiller P/E is about 4–5 percent. It is a bit tighter when the Shiller P/E is very high or low. This tightness could mean greater predictability at those times, but it could also be a bias from investors not seeing the true extremes possible in the distribution. Nonetheless, 4–5 percent is a lot for standard deviation, and it is big relative to the dispersion among all the forecasters at the forum. Bullish and bearish forecasters at the forum mostly did not differ from each other by more than one time-series standard deviation of 10-year returns. Thus, it will be very hard for anyone to claim a convincing victory!

The financial world, however, still demands a specific forecast, so I will oblige. Guesswork is always involved in making such a forecast, but the thought process around the guesswork can be interesting. I will forecast only the real (consumer price index–adjusted) return on the S&P 500, not the risk premium versus bonds. At the 2001 forum, we failed in deciding what benchmark to use in forecasting the equity risk premium, thus confusing the issue somewhat. In my view, our discussion was not meant to reflect differing bond forecasts; forecasting the real return on the S&P 500 is more to the point.

To do so, I like to start with the Shiller P/E, which was roughly 23.5 in early April 2011. I then reduce that number by 10 percent to get a measure of the current P/E using trend earnings (because earnings grow over time, the unmodified Shiller P/E is a lagging indicator of valuation). Doing so drops the Shiller P/E to about 21.5, which makes the earnings yield about 4.7 percent. To get a sustainable dividend yield, I cut the earnings yield figure in half to about 2.3 percent. Reducing the earnings yield reflects a historically reasonable payout ratio of about 50 percent, not the current payout ratio, which is lower. I am sneaking in some optimism by ignoring my own work with Arnott that shows growth is slower when payouts are low, as they are today. Next, I add about 1.5 percent for expected real growth in earnings. Using the Gordon growth model (Dividend/Price + Growth), the result is a long-term forecast real equity return of 3.8 percent.

Finally, I round to 4 percent (not to round is arrogantly overprecise!); that is my 10-year forecast, but with some more caveats. This rate assumes a steady state in the markets. That is, it assumes that the best forecast of the future Shiller P/E is the current Shiller P/E. A more pessimistic vision of the future would assume some regression to the long-run mean Shiller P/E, which is about 15. A very pessimistic vision of the future would assume a regression through the long-term mean, as some argue happens eventually after all bubbles. Aside from about three days in early 2009, and then only trivially, valuations have not been below historical means since well before 2000. But I am not that pessimistic.

I agree with others who have argued that valuations in the past were too low, partly because the returns that investors study are far more attainable today with diversified index funds. I think those at the forum in 2001 were just beginning to appreciate this argument, and it is one of the most important considerations when examining the historical ERP. Too often, investors take for granted that they can mimic the market's ERP by buying diversified index funds at very low fees. During much of the historical period, however, this option did not exist. Thus, investors today should require a lower total return, and pay a higher P/E, because they retain more of the return at lower risk. So, my forecast does not incorporate any mean reversion of P/Es. I will stick with a real 4 percent.

Although the journey to arrive at my forecast is messy, and as much art as science, I think the thought process is useful for investment managers.

REFERENCES

Arnott, Robert D., and Clifford S. Asness. 2003. "Surprise! Higher Dividends = Higher Earnings Growth." *Financial Analysts Journal*, vol. 59, no. 1 (January/February):70–87.

Equity Premiums around the World

Elroy Dimson
Leverhulme Emeritus Professor, London Business School
Visiting Professor of Finance, Cambridge Judge Business School

Paul Marsh
Emeritus Professor of Finance
London Business School

Mike Staunton
Director, London Share Price Database
London Business School

We update our global estimates of the historical equity risk premium that were first presented in *The Millennium Book: A Century of Investment Returns* (Dimson, Marsh, and Staunton 2000) and in *Triumph of the Optimists: 101 Years of Global Investment Returns* (Dimson, Marsh, and Staunton 2002). More detailed analysis is published in our annual volumes, the *Credit Suisse Global Investment Returns Yearbook* and the *Credit Suisse Global Investment Returns Sourcebook* (Dimson, Marsh, and Staunton 2011a and 2011b).

We provide estimates for 19 countries, including two North American markets (the United States and Canada), eight markets from what is now the euro currency area (Belgium, Finland, France, Germany, Ireland, Italy, the Netherlands, and Spain), five other European markets (Denmark, Norway, Sweden, Switzerland, and the United Kingdom), three Asia-Pacific markets (Japan, Australia, and New Zealand), and one African market (South Africa).

The Dimson–Marsh–Staunton (DMS) database, which is distributed by Morningstar, also includes six U.S. dollar–denominated regional indices (Dimson, Marsh, and Staunton 2011c). The indices are a 19-country World equity index, an 18-country World ex-U.S. equity index, a 13-country European equity index, and three corresponding government bond indices for the World, World ex-U.S., and Europe. For the equity indices, each country is weighted by market capitalization (or by GDP for the years before capitalizations were available). The bond indices are GDP weighted throughout.

Our dataset includes equities, long government bonds, bills, inflation, exchange rates, and GDP. More details about the data, the sources, and the index construction methods are presented in Dimson, Marsh, and Staunton (2008, 2011b).

Long-Run Global Returns

Investment returns can be extremely volatile. The 2000s were a period of disappointment for most equity investors, and few would extrapolate future returns from this recent experience. Including the 1990s adds a period of stock market exuberance that is also not indicative of expectations. To understand risk and return, long periods of history need to be examined. That is why we ensure that all our return series embrace 111 years of financial market history, from the start of 1900 to the end of 2010.

Panel A in **Figure 1** shows the cumulative total returns in nominal terms for U.S. equities, bonds, bills, and inflation for 1900–2010. Equities performed best, with an initial investment of $1 growing to $21,766 by year-end 2010. Long bonds and bills had lower returns, although they beat inflation. Their respective levels at the end of 2010 were $191 and $74, with the inflation index ending at $26. The legend shows the annualized returns were 9.4 percent for equities, 4.8 percent for bonds, and 3.9 percent for bills; inflation was 3.0 percent per year.

Because U.S. prices rose 26-fold over this period, it is helpful to compare returns in real terms. Panel B of Figure 1 shows the real returns on U.S. equities, bonds, and bills. Over the 111 years, an initial investment of $1 in equities, with dividends reinvested, would have grown in purchasing power by 851 times. The corresponding multiples for bonds and bills are 7.5 and 2.9 times the initial investment, respectively. As the legend shows, these terminal wealth figures correspond to annualized real returns of 6.3 percent for equities, 1.8 percent for bonds, and 1.0 percent for bills.

The United States is by far the world's best-documented capital market. Prior to the assembly of the DMS database, long-run evidence was invariably taken from U.S. markets and typically treated as being applicable universally. Few economies, if any, can rival the long-term growth of the United States, which makes it dangerous to generalize from U.S. historical returns. That is why we have put effort into documenting global investment returns.

Figure 2 shows annualized real equity, bond, and bill returns for 19 countries as well as the World, the World ex-U.S., and Europe indices. The countries and regions are ranked in ascending order of equity market performance. The real equity return was positive in every location, typically 3–6 percent per year. Equities were the best-performing asset class within every market. Furthermore, bonds performed better than bills in all the countries. This pattern of equities outperforming bonds, and of bonds outperforming bills, is precisely what we would expect because equities are riskier than bonds, whereas bonds are riskier than cash.

**Figure 1. Cumulative Returns on U.S. Equities,
Bonds, Bills, and Inflation, 1900–2010**

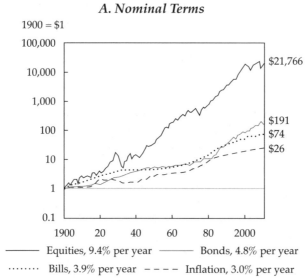

A. Nominal Terms

1900 = $1

Equities, 9.4% per year   Bonds, 4.8% per year

········ Bills, 3.9% per year   – – – – Inflation, 3.0% per year

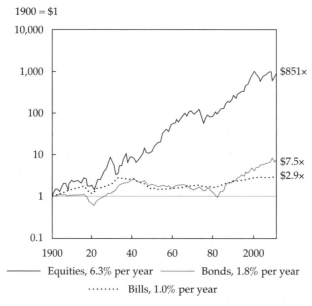

B. Real Terms

1900 = $1

Equities, 6.3% per year   Bonds, 1.8% per year

········ Bills, 1.0% per year

Source: Based on Dimson, Marsh, and Staunton (2002) and as updated in Dimson, Marsh, and Staunton (2011b).

Figure 2. Real Annualized Returns on Equities vs. Bonds and Bills Internationally, 1900–2010

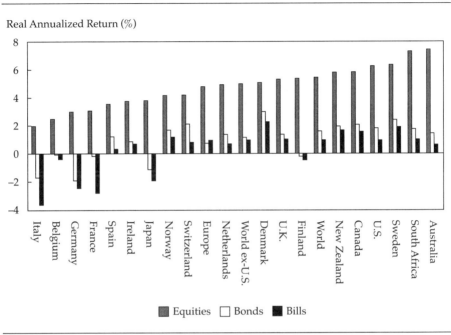

Source: Based on Dimson, Marsh, and Staunton (2002) and as updated in Dimson, Marsh, and Staunton (2011b).

Figure 2 also shows that although most countries' bonds had a positive real return, six countries experienced negative returns. With the exception of Finland, the latter were also among the worst equity performers. Mostly, their poor performance dates back to the first half of the 20th century, when these countries suffered most from the ravages of war and civil strife as well as periods of high inflation or hyperinflation associated with the wars and their aftermath.

The chart confirms that the United States performed well, ranking fourth for equity performance (real 6.3 percent per year) and sixth for bonds (real 1.8 percent per year). This result confirms the conjectures that U.S. returns would be high because the U.S. economy has been such an obvious success story and that it is unwise for investors to base their future projections solely on U.S. evidence. Figure 2 helps set this debate in context, however, by showing that although U.S. stocks did well, the United States was not the top performer nor were its returns especially high relative to the world averages. The real return on U.S. equities of 6.3 percent is more than a percentage point higher than the real U.S. dollar–denominated return of 5.0 percent on the World ex-U.S. index. A

35

common factor among the best-performing equity markets over the past 111 years is that they tended to be rich in resources and/or to be New World countries.

Table 1 provides statistics on real equity returns from 1900 to 2010. The geometric mean shows the 111-year annualized returns achieved by investors, and these are the figures that are plotted in Figure 2. The arithmetic mean shows the average of the 111 annual returns for each country or region. The arithmetic mean of a sequence of different returns is always larger than the geometric mean, and the more volatile the sequence of returns, the greater the gap between the arithmetic and geometric means. This fact is evident in the fifth column of Table 1, which shows the standard deviation of each equity market's annual returns.

The U.S. equity standard deviation of 20.3 percent places it at the lower end of the risk spectrum, ranking sixth after Canada (17.2 percent), Australia (18.2 percent), New Zealand (19.7 percent), Switzerland (19.8 percent), and the United Kingdom (20.0 percent). The World index has a standard deviation of just 17.7 percent, showing the risk reduction obtained from international diversification. The most volatile markets during this period are Germany (32.2 percent), Finland (30.3 percent), Japan (29.8 percent), and Italy (29.0 percent), which are the countries that were most affected by the world wars and inflation; Finland's case also reflects its heavy concentration in a single stock (Nokia) during recent periods. Additionally, Table 1 shows that, as one would expect, the countries with the highest standard deviations experienced the greatest range of returns—that is, the lowest minimum returns and the highest maximum returns.

Bear markets underline the risk of equities. Even in a less volatile market, such as the United States, losses can be huge. Table 1 shows that the worst calendar year for U.S. equities was 1931, with a real return of −38 percent. However, from peak to trough, U.S. equities fell by 79 percent in real terms during the 1929–31 Wall Street crash. The worst period for U.K. equities was the 1973–74 bear market, with stocks falling 71 percent in real terms and by 57 percent in a single year. More recently, 2008 had the dubious distinction of being the worst year on record for eight countries, the World index, the World ex-U.S., and Europe. The table shows that in several other countries, even more extreme returns have occurred, on both the downside and the upside.

Common-Currency Returns

So far, we have reported the real returns to a domestic equity investor based on local purchasing power in that investor's home country. For example, during 1900–2010, the annualized real return to a U.S. investor buying U.S. equities was 6.27 percent, whereas for a British investor buying U.K. equities, it was 5.33 percent. When considering cross-border investment, however, it is also

Table 1. Real (Inflation-Adjusted) Equity Returns around the World, 1900–2010

Country/Region	Geometric Mean (%)	Arithmetic Mean (%)	Standard Error (%)	Standard Deviation (%)	Minimum Return (%)	Year of Minimum	Maximum Return (%)	Year of Maximum
Australia	7.4	9.1	1.7	18.2	−42.5	2008	51.5	1983
Belgium	2.5	5.1	2.2	23.6	−57.1	2008	109.5	1940
Canada	5.9	7.3	1.6	17.2	−33.8	2008	55.2	1933
Denmark	5.-	6.9	2.0	20.9	−49.2	2008	107.8	1983
Finland	5.4	9.3	2.9	30.3	−60.8	1918	161.7	1999
France	3.-	5.7	2.2	23.5	−42.7	2008	66.1	1954
Germany	3.-	8.1	3.1	32.2	−90.8	1948	154.6	1949
Ireland	3.8	6.4	2.2	23.2	−65.4	2008	68.4	1977
Italy	2.0	6.1	2.8	29.0	−72.9	1945	120.7	1946
Japan	3.8	8.5	2.8	29.8	−85.5	1946	121.1	1952
Netherlands	5.0	7.1	2.1	21.8	−50.4	2008	101.6	1940
New Zealand	5.8	7.6	1.9	19.7	−54.7	1987	105.3	1983
Norway	4.2	7.2	2.6	27.4	−53.6	2008	166.9	1979
South Africa	7.3	9.5	2.1	22.6	−52.2	1920	102.9	1933
Spain	3.6	5.8	2.1	22.3	−43.3	1977	99.4	1986
Sweden	6.3	8.7	2.2	22.9	−43.6	1918	89.8	1905
Switzerland	4.2	6.1	1.9	19.8	−37.8	1974	59.4	1922
United Kingdom	5.3	7.2	1.9	20.0	−57.1	1974	96.7	1975
United States	6.3	8.3	1.9	20.3	−37.6	1931	56.3	1933
Europe	4.8	6.9	2.0	21.5	−46.6	2008	76.0	1933
World ex-U.S.	5.0	7.0	1.9	20.4	−43.3	2008	79.3	1933
World	5.5	7.0	1.7	17.7	−40.4	2008	69.9	1933

Source: Based on Dimson, Marsh, and Staunton (2002) and as updated in Dimson, Marsh, and Staunton (2011b).

necessary to account for exchange rate movements—for example, a U.S. investor buying U.K. equities or a U.K. investor buying U.S. equities. Each investor now has two exposures, one to foreign equities and the other to foreign currency, and each return needs to be converted into each investor's reference currency.

Rather than just comparing domestic returns, we translate all countries' local returns into a common currency. **Figure 3** shows the results of translating from the local currency to U.S. dollars. These dollar returns are expressed as real returns, adjusted for U.S. inflation. The gray bars show the annualized real domestic currency returns from 1900 to 2010, as presented earlier. The white bars are the common-currency returns, in real U.S. dollars, from the perspective of a U.S. investor. The black bars are the difference between the annualized real local-currency return and the annualized real dollar return. The black bars equate to the annualized inflation-adjusted exchange rate movement over the same period. The gap between the two return measures is less than 1 percent per annum for every country, indicating that purchasing power parity (PPP) held reasonably closely over the very long run (see Taylor 2002).

Figure 3. Real Annualized Equity Returns in Local Currency and U.S. Dollars, 1900–2010

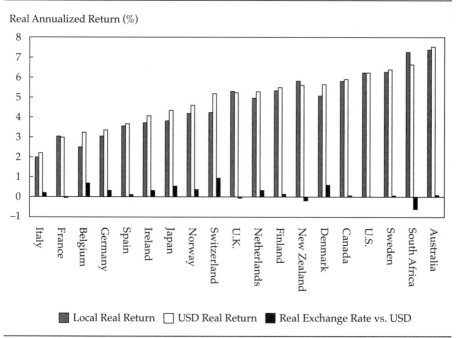

Source: Based on Dimson, Marsh, and Staunton (2002) and as updated in Dimson, Marsh, and Staunton (2011b).

In Figure 3, countries are ranked in ascending order based on the white bars, which show the annualized real dollar returns to a U.S. investor. Because PPP tends to hold, equity markets have a similar ranking whether they are ranked by domestic real returns or by their real dollar returns. Note that although the magnitude of the returns varies according to the choice of common currency, the rankings of the countries are the same regardless of which reference currency is used.

Worldwide Premium

Investment in equities has proven rewarding over the long run, but as we noted in Table 1, it has been accompanied by significant variability of returns. Investors do not like volatility—at least on the downside—and will be prepared to invest in riskier assets only if there is some compensation for this risk (for more on this subject, see Dimson, Marsh, and Staunton 2004). The reward for equity risk that investors have achieved in the past can be measured by comparing the return on equities with the return from risk-free investments, such as Treasury bills. The difference between equity and bill returns is known as the "equity risk premium." For long-term government bonds, the difference between bond and bill returns is referred to as the "maturity premium." Although our focus in this article is on the equity risk premium, we provide up-to-date evidence on the maturity premium in Dimson, Marsh, and Staunton (2011b).

We measure the historical equity risk premium by taking the geometric difference between the equity return and the risk-free return. The formula is

$$(1 + \text{Equity rate of return}) / (1 + \text{Risk-free return}) - 1.$$

For example, if we were evaluating stocks with a one-year return of 21 percent relative to T-bills yielding 10 percent, the realized equity risk premium would be 10 percent because $(1 + 21/100) / (1 + 10/100)$ is equal to $1 + 10/100$ and deducting 1 gives a premium of $10/100$, which is 10 percent. This measure of the risk premium is based on a ratio, and it thus has no numeraire. It is hence unaffected by whether returns are computed in dollars or pounds or euros or by whether returns are expressed in nominal or real terms.

Our preferred benchmark for the risk-free return is Treasury bills (i.e., very short-term, default-free, fixed-income government securities, or going back in history, the closest available equivalent in the years before T-bills became available). Many people, however, also measure the equity premium relative to long bonds, so we report both measures, even though bonds are clearly far from risk free in real terms. Detailed statistics on the equity risk premium relative to bills and bonds are given in **Table 2** and **Table 3**.

Table 2. Worldwide Equity Risk Premiums Relative to Bills, 1900–2010

Country/Region	Geometric Mean (%)	Arithmetic Mean (%)	Standard Error (%)	Standard Deviation (%)	Minimum Return (%)	Year of Minimum	Maximum Return (%)	Year of Maximum
Australia	6.7	8.3	1.7	17.6	−44.4	2008	49.2	1983
Belgium	2.9	5.5	2.3	24.7	−58.1	2008	130.4	1940
Canada	4.2	5.6	1.6	17.2	−34.7	2008	49.1	1933
Denmark	2.8	4.6	1.9	20.5	−50.6	2008	95.3	1983
Finland	5.9	9.5	2.9	30.2	−53.6	2008	159.2	1999
France	6.0	8.7	2.3	24.5	−44.8	2008	85.7	1941
Germany[a]	5.9	9.8	3.0	31.8	−45.3	2008	131.4	1949
Ireland	3.0	5.3	2.0	21.5	−66.7	2008	72.0	1977
Italy	5.8	9.8	3.0	32.0	−49.1	2008	150.3	1946
Japan	5.9	9.0	2.6	27.7	−48.3	1920	108.6	1952
Netherlands	4.2	6.5	2.2	22.8	−51.9	2008	126.7	1940
New Zealand	4.1	5.7	1.7	18.3	−58.3	1987	97.3	1983
Norway	3.0	5.9	2.5	26.5	−55.1	2008	157.1	1979
South Africa	6.2	8.3	2.1	22.1	−33.9	1920	106.2	1933
Spain	3.2	5.4	2.1	21.9	−39.9	2008	98.1	1986
Sweden	4.3	6.6	2.1	22.1	−41.3	2008	84.6	1905
Switzerland	3.4	5.1	1.8	18.9	−37.0	1974	54.8	1985
United Kingdom	4.3	6.0	1.9	19.9	−54.6	1974	121.8	1975
United States	5.3	7.2	1.9	19.8	−44.1	1931	56.6	1933
Europe	3.8	5.8	2.0	21.0	−47.4	2008	76.3	1933
World ex-U.S.	4.0	5.9	1.9	19.9	−44.2	2008	79.6	1933
World	4.5	5.9	1.6	17.1	−41.3	2008	70.3	1933

[a]All statistics for Germany are based on 109 years, excluding the hyperinflationary years of 1922–1923.

Source: Based on Dimson, Marsh, and Staunton (2002) and as updated in Dimson, Marsh, and Staunton (2011b).

Table 3. Worldwide Equity Risk Premiums Relative to Bonds, 1900–2010

Country/Region	Geometric Mean (%)	Arithmetic Mean (%)	Standard Error (%)	Standard Deviation (%)	Minimum Return (%)	Year of Minimum	Maximum Return (%)	Year of Maximum
Australia	5.9	7.8	1.9	19.8	−52.9	2008	66.3	1980
Belgium	2.6	4.9	2.0	21.4	−60.3	2008	84.4	1940
Canada	3.7	5.3	1.7	18.2	−40.7	2008	48.6	1950
Denmark	2.0	3.4	1.6	17.2	−54.3	2008	74.9	1972
Finland	5.6	9.2	2.9	30.3	−56.3	2008	173.1	1999
France	3.2	5.6	2.2	22.9	−50.3	2008	84.3	1946
Germany[a]	5.4	8.8	2.7	28.4	−50.8	2008	116.6	1949
Ireland	2.9	4.9	1.9	19.8	−66.6	2008	83.2	1972
Italy	3.7	7.2	2.8	29.6	−49.4	2008	152.2	1946
Japan	5.0	9.1	3.1	32.8	−45.2	2008	193.0	1948
Netherlands	3.5	5.8	2.1	22.2	−55.6	2008	107.6	1940
New Zealand	3.8	5.4	1.7	18.1	−59.7	1987	72.7	1983
Norway	2.5	5.5	2.7	28.0	−57.8	2008	192.1	1979
South Africa	5.5	7.2	1.9	19.6	−34.3	2008	70.9	1979
Spain	2.3	4.3	2.0	20.8	−42.7	2008	69.1	1986
Sweden	3.8	6.1	2.1	22.3	−48.1	2008	87.5	1905
Switzerland	2.1	3.6	1.7	17.6	−40.6	2008	52.2	1985
United Kingdom	3.9	5.2	1.6	17.0	−38.4	2008	80.8	1975
United States	4.4	6.4	1.9	20.5	−50.1	2008	57.2	1933
Europe	3.9	5.2	1.6	16.6	−47.6	2008	67.9	1923
World ex-U.S.	3.3	5.0	1.5	15.5	−47.1	2008	51.7	1923
World	3.3	5.0	1.5	15.5	−47.9	2008	38.3	1954

[a]All statistics for Germany are based on 109 years, excluding the hyperinflationary years of 1922–1923.

Source: Based on Dimson, Marsh, and Staunton (2002) and as updated in Dimson, Marsh, and Staunton (2011b).

The estimates in Table 2 and Table 3 are lower than frequently quoted historical averages, such as the Ibbotson Yearbook (2011) figures for the United States and the earlier Barclays Capital (1999) studies for the United Kingdom. The differences arise from a bias (subsequently corrected) in the construction of the U.K. index used in Barclays' studies and, for both countries, our use of a long time frame (1900–2010) that incorporates the earlier part of the 20th century as well as the opening years of the 21st century, utilizing data described in Dimson, Marsh, and Staunton (2008). Our global focus also results in lower risk premiums than previously assumed. Prior views have been heavily influenced by the experience of the United States, whereas the view expressed here reflects an average of 19 countries, of which the United States is only one and in which the U.S. risk premium is somewhat higher than average.

The annualized equity premiums for the 19 countries and the World indices are summarized in **Figure 4**, in which countries are ranked according to the equity premium measured relative to bills, displayed as bars. The line plot presents each country's corresponding risk premium, measured relative to bonds. Over the entire 111 years, the annualized (geometric) equity risk premium, relative to bills, is 5.3 percent for the United States and 4.3 percent for the United Kingdom. Averaged across all 19 countries, the risk premium relative to bills is 4.6 percent, whereas the risk premium on the World equity index is 4.5 percent. Relative to long-term government bonds, the story is similar. The annualized U.S. equity risk premium relative to bonds is 4.4 percent and the corresponding figure for the United Kingdom is 3.9 percent. Across all 19 markets, the risk premium relative to bonds averages 3.8 percent; for the World index, it is also 3.8 percent.

Survivorship Bias

For the World index, our estimate of the annualized historical equity premium relative to bills is 4.5 percent. This estimate is based on the 19 countries in the DMS database, all of which survived from 1900 to 2011. These 19 countries accounted for an estimated 89 percent of the world equity market in 1900. The remaining 11 percent came from markets that existed in 1900 but for which we have been unable to obtain data. Some of these omitted markets failed to survive, and in cases like Russia in 1917 and China in 1949, investors lost all of their money. To quantify the maximum possible impact of omitted markets on the magnitude of the historical equity risk premium, we make an extreme assumption. We assume that all omitted markets became valueless and that this outcome occurred for every omitted country in a single disastrous year, rather than building up gradually. We then ask what risk premium investors would have earned if in 1900, they had purchased a holding in the entire World

Figure 4. Worldwide Annualized Equity Risk Premium Relative to Bills and Bonds, 1900–2010

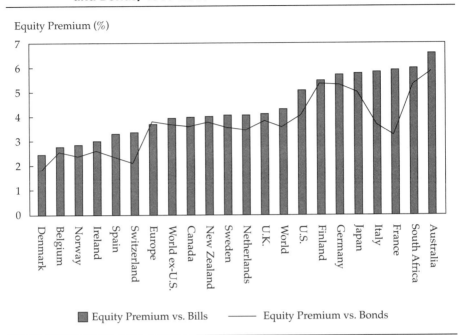

Note: Statistics for Germany are based on 109 years, excluding the hyperinflationary years of 1922–1923.
Source: Based on Dimson, Marsh, and Staunton (2002) and as updated in Dimson, Marsh, and Staunton (2011b).

market, including countries omitted from the DMS database, and held this portfolio for 111 years. At the start of the period, their portfolio would have comprised an 89 percent holding in the DMS World index and an 11 percent holding in countries that we have assumed were all destined to become valueless.

Given these extreme assumptions, we demonstrate (see Dimson, Marsh, and Staunton 2008) that survivorship bias could, at most, give rise to an overstatement of the geometric mean risk premium on the World equity index by about one-tenth of a percentage point. If omitted markets did not all become valueless—and we know that very many did not—the magnitude of survivorship bias would be smaller still. Although debate continues about the precise impact of the bias because some, but not all, of these equity markets experienced a total loss of value, the net impact on the worldwide geometric mean equity premium is no more than 0.1 percent. The effect on the arithmetic mean is similar. The intuition involves the disappearance of 11 percent of the value of the market over 111 years, which represents a loss of value averaging 0.1 percent per year. We conclude that survivorship bias in world stock market returns is negligible.

Decomposing the Equity Risk Premium

Many people argue that the historical equity premium is a reasonable guide to what to expect in the future. Their reasoning is that over the long run, investors should expect good luck to balance out bad luck. If this view is correct, then the average premium investors receive should be close to the premium they required and "priced in" before the event. But even over a period as long as 111 years, this expectation may fail to be the case. It is possible that investors have enjoyed more than their share of good luck, making the past too good to last. If so, the historical premium would reflect "the triumph of the optimists" and would overstate expectations.

As an alternative approach, we seek to infer what investors may have been expecting, on average, in the past. To understand investors' expectations, we separate the historical equity premium into elements that correspond to investor expectations and elements of non-repeatable good or bad luck. In our article "The Worldwide Equity Premium: A Smaller Puzzle" (Dimson, Marsh, and Staunton 2008), we show that the equity premium can be decomposed into five components: the annualized mean dividend yield, plus the annualized growth rate of real dividends, plus the annualized expansion over time of the price/ dividend ratio, plus the annualized change in the real exchange rate, minus the real risk-free rate.

Of these components, the dividend yield has been the dominant factor historically. At first sight, this may seem surprising because on a daily basis, investors' interest tends to focus mainly on the capital gains element of returns, such as stock price fluctuations and market movements. Indeed, over a single year, equities are so volatile that most of an investor's performance is attributable to capital gains or losses. Dividend income adds a relatively modest amount to each year's gain or loss. But although year-to-year performance is driven by capital appreciation, long-run returns are heavily influenced by reinvested dividends.

The difference in terminal wealth that results from reinvested dividend income is very large. As Figure 1 shows, the total real return from investing $1 in U.S. equities at the start of 1900—and reinvesting all dividend income—is an annualized 6.3 percent, such that by the start of 2011, the initial investment would have grown in purchasing power by 851 times. If dividends had not been reinvested, the initial $1 investment would have grown in purchasing power by just 8.5 times, equivalent to a real capital gain of 1.9 percent per year over the 111 years. A portfolio of U.S. equities with dividends reinvested would have grown to 100 times the value it would have attained if dividends had been spent. The longer the investment horizon, the more important dividend income becomes. For the seriously long-term investor, the value of a portfolio corresponds closely to the present value of dividends.

Components of the Equity Premium

To quantify the components of the equity premium, we examine the decomposition for all 19 countries and the World index over 1900–2010. The results are presented in **Table 4**, and we examine each component in turn. The second column of the table shows the annualized dividend yield for each market, reinforcing the point that the dividend yield has been the dominant factor historically. Across all 19 countries, the mean yield was 4.5 percent, although it was as large as 5.8 percent (South Africa) and as low as 3.5 percent (Switzerland). The annualized dividend yield for the United States (4.2 percent)

Table 4. Decomposition of the Historical Equity Risk Premium, 1900–2010

Country/Region	Geometric Mean Dividend Yield	*plus* Real Dividend Growth Rate	*plus* Expansion in the P/D Ratio	*plus* Change in Real Exchange Rate	*minus* U.S. Real Interest Rate	*equals* Equity Premium for U.S. Investors
Australia	5.76	1.10	0.48	0.10	0.96	6.53
Belgium	3.72	−1.48	0.36	0.70	0.96	2.28
Canada	4.39	0.84	0.56	0.09	0.96	4.94
Denmark	4.58	−1.13	1.64	0.57	0.96	4.69
Finland	4.76	0.49	0.09	0.15	0.96	4.53
France	3.81	−0.90	0.18	−0.04	0.96	2.05
Germany	3.66	−1.16	0.58	0.31	0.96	2.40
Ireland	4.57	−0.94	0.16	0.31	0.96	3.09
Italy	4.06	−1.52	−0.47	0.20	0.96	1.24
Japan	5.22	−2.39	1.08	0.54	0.96	3.39
Netherlands	4.94	−0.51	0.55	0.35	0.96	4.34
New Zealand	5.38	1.26	−0.84	−0.21	0.96	4.60
Norway	4.00	−0.13	0.33	0.38	0.96	3.62
South Africa	5.82	0.95	0.46	−0.61	0.96	5.65
Spain	4.18	−0.60	0.01	0.12	0.96	2.71
Sweden	4.02	1.77	0.43	0.09	0.96	5.41
Switzerland	3.48	0.46	0.28	0.91	0.96	4.22
United Kingdom	4.63	0.46	0.20	−0.06	0.96	4.27
United States	4.24	1.37	0.56	0.00	0.96	5.26
Average	4.49	−0.11	0.35	0.21	0.96	3.96
Standard dev.	0.69	1.18	0.51	0.35	0.00	1.39
World (USD)	4.11	0.83	0.48	0.00	0.96	4.49

Notes: Premiums are relative to bills. Summations and subtractions are geometric.

Source: Based on Dimson, Marsh, and Staunton (2008) and as updated in Dimson, Marsh, and Staunton (2011b).

was close to the cross-sectional average. For the World index, the annualized dividend yield was 4.1 percent, which is 3.1 percent higher than the real risk-free return from Treasury bills (see the penultimate column).

The real dividend growth rates in the third column of Table 4 reveal that in most markets, real dividend growth was lower than it was in the United States. In more than half of the countries, real dividends declined, and only four countries enjoyed real dividend growth of more than 1 percent per year. The equal-weighted average rate of real dividend growth across the 19 countries was slightly negative, although the World index's real dividend growth rate was 0.83 percent, bolstered by its heavy U.S. weighting. Dividends, and probably earnings, barely outpaced inflation. Over sufficiently long intervals, higher equity returns are generally associated with higher profits, which, in turn, generate larger dividends; comparing real equity returns (Table 1) with real dividend growth rates (Table 4) reveals a strong correlation (0.82) between the two.

The fourth column shows the expansion in the price-to-dividend ratio (P/D). Superior stock market performance and the magnitude of the historical equity risk premium are sometimes attributed to the expansion of valuation ratios, but the importance of this can be overstated. Table 4 shows that over the last 111 years, the P/D rose (dividend yields have fallen) in all but two countries, whereas the P/D of the World index grew by 0.48 percent per year. There are two possible explanations for this long-term decline in dividend yields: It may represent a repricing of equities (a downward shift in the capitalization rate or an upward shift in growth expectations), or the average payout ratio may have declined. In *Triumph of the Optimists* (Dimson, Marsh, and Staunton 2002), we note that equities enjoyed a rerating over this period but that in some countries, especially the United States, there were well-known changes in the cash distribution policies of corporations that made it necessary to take into account the impact of repurchases as well as cash dividends. The long-term multiple expansion of 0.48 percent per year is modest, however, given the improved opportunities for stock market diversification that took place over this period.

The fifth column shows the long-term change in the real (inflation-adjusted) exchange rate. As noted earlier, to examine the equity premium from the perspective of a global investor located in a specific home country, such as the United States, the real, local-currency returns need to be converted to real, common-currency returns. The annualized change in the 19 countries' real exchange rates averages only 0.21 percent per year, so this effect is small. As noted earlier, every country's real exchange rate change was within the range of ±1 percent.

46

The penultimate column is the historical real U.S. risk-free interest rate, and the final column computes the historical annualized equity premium for all the markets from the perspective of a U.S. investor. The realized equity premium relative to bills was, on average, 4.0 percent, with a cross-sectional standard deviation of 1.4 percent. For the U.S. dollar–denominated World index, the realized equity premium relative to bills was 4.5 percent (see the final entry in the bottom row of Table 4).

Investor Expectations

Over the long term, purchasing power parity has been a good indicator of long-run exchange rate changes (for more information, see Taylor 2002 and Dimson, Marsh, and Staunton 2011b, p. 19). The contribution to equity returns of real exchange rate changes is, therefore, an unanticipated windfall. It implies an upward bias of 0.21 percent in the cross-sectional average of the country equity premiums (there is no bias for the World index because it is denominated in the reference currency). Furthermore, as noted by Grinold, Kroner, and Siegel in their paper in this book, valuation ratios cannot be expected to expand indefinitely. Consequently, the contribution to equity returns of repricing is also likely to have been unanticipated; it implies an upward bias of 0.35 percent in the cross-sectional average of the country equity premiums and of 0.48 percent for the World index. Together, these two adjustments cause the equity premium to decline from 4.0 percent to 3.4 percent for the average country and from 4.5 percent to 4.0 percent for the World index.

In the sample of 19 countries, the average country had a long-term real dividend growth rate of slightly less than zero. In the World index, dividends outpaced inflation by an annual 0.8 percent, bolstered by the heavy weighting of the United States, where real dividends grew by 1.4 percent. But the 111-year annualized growth rate conceals a game of two halves. The 20th century opened with much promise, and only a pessimist would have believed that the next half-century would involve widespread civil and international wars, the Wall Street crash, the Great Depression, episodes of hyperinflation, the spread of communism, and the start of the Cold War. During 1900–1949, the annualized real return on the World equity index was 3.4 percent. By 1950, only a rampant optimist would have dreamed that during the following half-century, the annualized real return would be 9 percent. Yet, the second half of the 20th century was a period when many events turned out better than expected: There was no third world war, the Cuban missile crisis was defused, the Berlin Wall fell, the Cold War ended, productivity and efficiency accelerated, technology progressed, economic development spread from a few industrial countries to most of the world, and governance became stockholder driven.

The 9 percent annualized real return on world equities during 1950–1999 almost certainly exceeded expectations and more than compensated for the poor first half of the 20th century.

The question now is, What real dividend growth can be projected for the future? Pessimists may favor a figure of much less than the 0.8 percent historical average on the grounds that the "good luck" after 1950 more than outweighed the "bad luck" before 1950. Optimists may foresee indefinite real growth of 2 percent or more. Ilmanen (2011, p. 58) argues for a forward-looking approach. The yield on the World index as of year-end 2010 was 2.5 percent, well below the long-run historical average. If we assume future real dividend growth of 2 percent from this lower starting point, then the prospective premium on the World index declines to 3–3.5 percent, depending on the assumption made about the expected future real risk-free rate. The corresponding arithmetic mean risk premium would be around 4.5–5 percent, as we explained in Dimson, Marsh, and Staunton (2008). Our estimate of the expected long-run equity risk premium is less than the historical premium and much less than the premium in the second half of the 20th century. Many investment books still cite figures as high as 7 percent for the geometric mean and 9 percent for the arithmetic mean, but investors who rely on such numbers are likely to be disappointed.

Time-Varying Risk Premiums

The equity premium should be higher at times when the equity market is riskier and/or when investors are more risk averse. Yet, when markets are very volatile, extensive empirical evidence indicates that volatility tends to revert quite rapidly to the mean (for more information, see Dimson, Marsh, and Staunton 2011b, p. 34). We can, therefore, expect the period of extreme volatility to be short-lived, elevating the expected equity premium only over the relatively short run. But the premium may also vary with changes in investors' risk aversion. The latter will naturally vary among individuals and institutions and will be linked to life cycles as well as wealth levels.

The links between wealth levels and risk aversion suggest that there will be periods when risk aversion will be more or less than its long-run average. Particularly after sharp market declines, investors in aggregate will be poorer and more risk averse. At such times, markets are also typically more volatile and highly leveraged. Investors will thus demand a higher risk premium, which will drive markets even lower. Stocks are then priced to give a higher future expected return. So on average, achieved returns should be higher after market declines. The reverse logic applies following bull markets; when investors are richer, then risk aversion and, hence, the equity premium are expected to be lower.

Therefore, equity markets might be expected to exhibit mean reversion, with higher returns typically following market declines and lower returns, on average, following market rises. If there is appreciable mean reversion, then a market-timing strategy based on, for example, buying stocks after large price drops (or when market dividend yields are high or price-to-earnings ratios are low) and selling stocks after significant market rises should generate higher absolute returns. This rational economic explanation for mean reversion is based on time-varying equity premiums and discount rates. The more widely held view among investment practitioners, however, is that equity markets exhibit mean reversion for behavioral reasons—namely, that markets overreact. It is believed that in down markets, fear and over-pessimism drive prices too low, whereas in up markets, irrational exuberance and over-optimism cause markets to rise too high. In both cases, there will eventually be a correction so that equity markets mean revert.

A key difference between the rational economic view and the behavioral view is that if the former is correct, investors simply expect to earn a fair reward at all times for the risks involved. Thus, although market-timing strategies might seem to increase returns *ex post*, these higher *ex post* returns may simply reflect a realization of the higher *ex ante* returns required to compensate investors for additional risk. Put another way, the good news is that short-term expected returns are likely to be higher after market declines. The bad news is that volatility and risk aversion are correspondingly higher, and larger returns are needed to compensate for this increase. Loading up on equities at these risky times may take courage, but if subsequent returns prove to be higher, this outcome is a reward for risk, not for timing skill.

The problem with both the rational economic and behavioral views is that the evidence for mean reversion is weak. Mean reversion would imply that the equity premium is to some extent predictable, that risk over the long run is less than short-run volatility suggests, and that investors with a long horizon should favor equities compared with short-horizon investors. Yet, despite extensive research, this debate is far from settled. In a special issue of the *Review of Financial Studies*, leading scholars expressed opposing views, with Cochrane (2008) and Campbell and Thompson (2008) arguing for predictability, whereas Welch and Goyal (2008, p. 1455) find that "these models would not have helped an investor with access only to available information to profitably time the market." Cochrane's (2011) recent Presidential Address demonstrates the persistence of this controversy.

As we pointed out in our article (Dimson, Marsh, and Staunton 2004), and as articulated more formally by Pástor and Stambaugh (Forthcoming), mean reversion (if it exists) does not make equities safer in the long run. The reason is that there are three additional components of long-term risk that pull in the opposite direction. For example, an investor does not know what the average stock market return is going to be in the future, nor what the equity premium is today, nor what the other parameters of the return process are. These issues leave the investor with substantial estimation risk, and all three components of uncertainty get bigger as the investment horizon lengthens. As a result, Pástor and Stambaugh conclude that on a forward-looking basis, stocks are more risky over the long run. Diris (2011) elaborates on this view and points out that although stocks can be safer over long investment horizons, provided markets are fairly stable, they are riskier when held for the long term over periods that suffer from financial crises or other turmoil.

In summary, although some experts say that knowledge of current and recent market conditions can improve market timing, others conclude that investors cannot do better than to forecast that the future equity premium will resemble the (long-term) past. Moreover, although a lot of money could be earned if investors managed to invest at the bottom of the market, sadly the bottom can be identified only in hindsight. There are, of course, good reasons to expect the equity premium to vary over time. Market volatility clearly fluctuates, and investors' risk aversion also varies over time. But although sharply lower (or higher) stock prices may have an impact on immediate returns, the effect on long-term performance will be diluted. Moreover, volatility does not usually stay at abnormally high levels for long, and investor sentiment is also mean reverting. For practical purposes, therefore, and consistent with our discussion here, we conclude that when forecasting the long-run equity premium, it is hard to improve on evidence that reflects the longest worldwide history that is available at the time the forecast is being made.

Conclusion

Our approach is based on analyzing a comprehensive database of annual asset class returns from the beginning of 1900 to the end of 2010 and estimating realized returns and equity premiums for 19 national markets and three regions. Our estimates, including those for the United States and the United Kingdom, are lower than some frequently quoted historical averages. Yet, we find that the equity premium is positive and substantial in all markets and that survivorship bias has had only a very small effect on the estimate of the premium for the World index.

The historical equity premiums, presented here as annualized (i.e., geometric mean) estimates, are equal to investors' *ex ante* expectations plus the effect of luck. The worldwide historical premium was larger than investors are likely to have anticipated because of such factors as unforeseen exchange rate gains and unanticipated expansion in valuation multiples. In addition, past returns were also enhanced during the second half of the 20th century by business conditions that improved in many dimensions. We infer that investors expect a long-run equity premium (relative to bills) of around 3–3.5 percent on a geometric mean basis and, by implication, an arithmetic mean premium for the World index of approximately 4.5–5 percent. From a long-term historical and global perspective, the equity premium is smaller than was once thought. The equity premium survives as a puzzle, however, and we have no doubt that it will continue to intrigue finance scholars in the foreseeable future.

Elroy Dimson thanks the Leverhulme Trust, and all three authors thank the Credit Suisse Research Institute for its support.

REFERENCES

Barclays Capital. 1999. *Equity Gilt Study*. London: Barclays Bank PLC.

Campbell, John Y., and Samuel B. Thompson. 2008. "Predicting Excess Stock Returns Out of Sample: Can Anything Beat the Historical Average?" *Review of Financial Studies*, vol. 21, no. 4 (July):1509–1531.

Cochrane, John. 2008. "The Dog That Did Not Bark: A Defense of Return Predictability." *Review of Financial Studies*, vol. 21, no. 4 (July):1533–1575.

———. 2011. "Presidential Address: Discount Rates." *Journal of Finance*, vol. 66, no. 4 (August):1047–1108.

Dimson, Elroy, Paul Marsh, and Mike Staunton. 2000. *The Millennium Book: A Century of Investment Returns*. London: ABN-Amro and London Business School.

———. 2002. *Triumph of the Optimists: 101 Years of Global Investment Returns*. Princeton, NJ: Princeton University Press.

———. 2004. "Irrational Optimism." *Financial Analysts Journal*, vol. 60, no. 1 (January/February):15–25.

———. 2008. "The Worldwide Equity Premium: A Smaller Puzzle." In *The Handbook of the Equity Risk Premium*. Edited by Rajnish Mehra. Amsterdam: Elsevier.

———. 2011a. *Credit Suisse Global Investment Returns Yearbook 2011*. Zurich: Credit Suisse Research Institute.

———. 2011b. *Credit Suisse Global Investment Returns Sourcebook 2011*. Zurich: Credit Suisse Research Institute.

———. 2011c. *The Dimson–Marsh–Staunton Global Investment Returns Database*. New York: Morningstar, Inc.

Diris, Bart. 2011. "Model Uncertainty for Long-Term Investors." Erasmus University Rotterdam working paper presented at the 38th Annual Meetings of the European Finance Association, Stockholm (August).

Ibbotson/Morningstar. 2011. *Ibbotson SBBI Classic Yearbook*. Chicago: Ibbotson/Morningstar.

Ilmanen, Antti. 2011. *Expected Returns: An Investor's Guide to Harvesting Market Rewards*. Chichester, U.K.: John Wiley & Sons.

Pástor, Luboš, and Robert F. Stambaugh. Forthcoming. "Are Stocks Really Less Volatile in the Long Run?" *Journal of Finance*.

Taylor, Alan M. 2002. "A Century of Purchasing-Power Parity." *Review of Economics and Statistics*, vol. 84, no. 1 (February):139–150.

Welch, Ivo, and Amit Goyal. 2008. "A Comprehensive Look at the Empirical Performance of Equity Premium Prediction." *Review of Financial Studies*, vol. 21, no. 4 (July):1455–1508.

A Supply Model of the Equity Premium

Richard C. Grinold
Former Managing Director
Barclays Global Investors

Kenneth F. Kroner
Managing Director
BlackRock

Laurence B. Siegel
Research Director, Research Foundation of CFA Institute
Senior Advisor, Ounavarra Capital LLC

The equity risk premium (ERP) is almost certainly the most important variable in finance. It tells you how much you need to save, how much you can spend, and how to allocate your assets between equities and bonds. Yet, recognized experts cannot agree on the ERP's value within an order of magnitude or even agree whether it is negative or positive. At a 2001 symposium, the predecessor of the one documented in this book, Robert Arnott and Ronald Ryan set forth an ERP estimate of −0.9 percent and Roger Ibbotson and Peng Chen proposed +6 percent.[1] The estimates in this book are much more tightly clustered, but considerable disagreement remains about how to estimate the premium as well as its size.

Grinold and Kroner (2002) proposed a model of the ERP that linked equity returns to gross domestic product (GDP) growth.[2] The key insight, which draws on earlier work by a number of authors, was that aggregate corporate profits cannot grow indefinitely much faster—or much slower—than GDP. (And as Herbert Stein was fond of reminding us, any economic trend that cannot continue forever will not.) If profits grow faster than GDP, they eventually take over the economy, leaving nothing for labor, government, natural resource owners, or other claimants. If profits grow more slowly than

---

[1]See Arnott and Ryan (2001); Ibbotson and Chen (2003). The Ibbotson and Chen estimate of 6 percent is an arithmetic mean expectation; their geometric mean expectation was 4 percent.

[2]A second printing of this article, from March 2004, is available online at www.cfapubs.org/userimages/ContentEditor/1141674677679/equity_risk_premium.pdf.

GDP, they eventually disappear and businesses will have no profit motive to continue operating. Thus, in the very long run, the ratio of profits to GDP is roughly constant.

The title of this paper, a shortened and updated version of Grinold and Kroner (2002), refers to the "supply model" of Diermeier, Ibbotson, and Siegel (1984), who differentiated between the demand for capital market returns (what investors need to compensate them for risk) and the supply of returns (what the macroeconomy makes available). The original supply model likewise made use of a link between profits and GDP. Grinold and Kroner (2002) was titled "The Equity Risk Premium: Analyzing the Long-Run Prospects for the Stock Market," but the similarity with the title of this book forced us to rename the current paper. Although our method is designed to produce an ERP estimate that reflects both supply and demand, the link to macroeconomic performance gives it a supply-side flavor.[3]

When we revisited the estimates from Grinold and Kroner (2002), we found that not all the components could be updated with equal accuracy, so the ERP estimate provided here is subject to some important caveats regarding data adequacy. The method that we recommend, however, remains largely unchanged from Grinold and Kroner (2002).

The Equity Risk Premium Model

We define the equity risk premium as the expected total return differential between the S&P 500 Index and a 10-year par U.S. government bond over the next 10 years. Our forecast of the return to the 10-year government bond over the next 10 years is simply the yield on that bond. Therefore, the ERP becomes

$$E\left(R_S - R_B\right) = \text{Expected S\&P 500 return} - \text{10-year bond yield.} \tag{1}$$

A purer and more "modern" approach is to conduct the whole analysis in real terms and to use the yield on a 10-year par Treasury Inflation-Protected Securities (TIPS) bond or, alternatively, a 10-year TIPS strip as the relevant bond yield. The authors of some of the other papers in this book do just that. We estimate the ERP over 10-year nominal bonds, however, because that is what Grinold and Kroner (2002) did. The numerical difference between the results of the two methods, real and nominal, is not large.

Forecasting the return on the S&P 500 over the next 10 years is more difficult and, therefore, gets most of the attention in this paper. The framework we use is to decompose equity returns into several understandable pieces and then examine each piece separately.

---

[3] A more detailed history of the estimation of the ERP can be found in the foreword (by Laurence B. Siegel) in Kaplan (2011).

The return to equities over a single period can always be broken down as

$$R_S = \text{Income return} + \text{Nominal earnings growth} + \text{Repricing}. \tag{2}$$

The income return is the percentage of market value that is distributed to shareholders as cash. If dividends are the only source of income, then the income return is equivalent to the dividend yield. Today, share repurchase programs (buybacks) are another common means of distributing cash to shareholders. Cash takeovers (by one company of another) should also be counted in the income return of an index that includes the stock of the acquired company.

The next two terms in Equation 2 represent the capital gain. Capital gains come from a combination of earnings growth and P/E expansion or contraction, which we call "repricing."

For expository purposes, we decompose the components further and use more precise notation. The return over a single period is

$$R = \underbrace{\frac{D}{P} - \Delta S}_{\text{Income}} + \underbrace{i + g}_{\text{Earnings growth}} + \underbrace{\Delta PE}_{\text{Repricing}}. \tag{3}$$

The first term, D/P, is simply the dividend yield. The second term, $-\Delta S$, is the percentage change in the number of shares outstanding. The percentage change in the number of shares outstanding equals the "repurchase yield" (which theoretically also includes cash takeovers) minus new shares issued (dilution); it has a negative sign because a decrease in the number of shares outstanding adds to return and an increase subtracts from return.[4] Together, the terms D/P and $-\Delta S$ measure the fraction of market capitalization that the companies in an index, in aggregate, return to shareholders in cash. Therefore, we refer to the sum of these two terms as the "income return."

The remaining terms, $i + g + \Delta PE$, make up the capital gain. The term i represents the inflation rate. The term g is the real earnings (not earnings per share) growth rate over the period of measurement. The final term, ΔPE, is the percentage change in the P/E multiple over the period. We refer to this last piece as the "repricing" part of the return.

---

[4]Share buybacks may be viewed as either a component of income return or a component of capital gain. An owner of a single share who holds on to the share through the share buyback program experiences the buyback as a component of capital gain because the same earnings are divided among fewer shares, which causes EPS to rise although earnings (not per share) have not changed. If the stock's P/E and all other factors are held equal, then the stock price rises. An index fund investor, however, experiences the share buyback as cash income because the index fund manager—who tenders some of the shares to the issuer to keep the stock's (now decreased) weight in the fund proportionate to its weight in the index—receives cash, which is then distributed to, or held by, fund shareholders like any other cash (tax considerations aside). We choose to view share buybacks as a component of income return.

It is important to realize that this decomposition of returns is essentially an identity, not an assumption, *so any view on the equity risk premium can be mapped into these components.* To illustrate, if the current 10-year bond yield is 3 percent, anyone who believes that the ERP is currently 4 percent must believe that the income return, nominal earnings growth, and repricing sum to 7 percent.

Historical Returns

Let us briefly consider what risk premium markets have provided historically. Over the last 85 years (1926–2010), the U.S. stock market and the intermediate-term U.S. Treasury bond market have delivered compound annual nominal returns of 9.9 percent and 5.4 percent, respectively.[5] Thus, the realized premium that stocks delivered over bonds was 4.5 percent.[6] The historical return decomposition in **Table 1** can be used to better understand this 9.9 percent annual equity return.

The income return (through dividends only, not share buybacks) on the S&P 500 was 4.1 percent annualized over this 85-year period. In this decomposition, we adjusted earnings growth for increases in the number of shares to arrive at *earnings per share (EPS) growth.* EPS grew at a rate of about 4.9 percent per year (1.9 percent real growth and 3.0 percent inflation) over the period.

Table 1. Decomposition of Total Returns on the S&P 500,[a] 1926–2010

Income return	4.10%
Real EPS growth	1.91
Inflation	2.99
P/E repricing	0.58
Within-year reinvestment return[b]	0.28
Total return	9.87%

[a]S&P 90 from January 1926 to February 1957; S&P 500 from March 1957 to 2010.
[b]Reinvestment of dividends paid during the year in the capital gain index (which consists of real EPS growth plus inflation plus P/E repricing).
Source: Morningstar/Ibbotson (used by permission).

---

[5] See the data for large-company stocks (i.e., the S&P 90 from January 1926 through February 1957 and the S&P 500 thereafter) in Table 2.1 in Ibbotson SBBI (2011, p. 32). Returns are before fees, transaction costs, taxes, and other costs.

[6] This amount is the arithmetic difference of geometric means. The geometric difference of geometric means, or the compound annual rate at which stocks outperformed bonds, is given by $(1 + 0.099)/(1 + 0.054) - 1 = 4.27$ percent.

The remainder of the total return on equities was due to repricing. The P/E of the market, measured as the end-of-year price divided by trailing 12-month earnings, grew from 11.3 at year-end 1925 to 18.5 at year-end 2010.[7] This repricing works out to an additional return, or P/E expansion, of 0.58 percent per year. A common view is that this P/E expansion was understandable and reasonable in light of the technological and financial innovations over this long period. For example, accounting standards became more transparent (recent "fraud stocks" notwithstanding). Such innovations as the index fund made it easier for investors to diversify security-specific risk and to save on costs. Mutual fund complexes provided easier access to institutional-quality active management. Finally, many market observers perceive the business cycle to have been under better control in recent decades than it was in the 1920s and 1930s, which made expected earnings smoother; the recent near depression and quick recovery, at least in corporate profits and the stock market, support this view somewhat. All these factors have made equity investing less risky and contributed to the repricing over this 85-year period.

But the presence of these factors in the past does not mean that we should build continued upward repricing into our forecasts. We consider this issue later in this paper.

Chart 1 of Grinold and Kroner (2002) further dissects the return decomposition into annual return contributions. Their graph demonstrates that the noisiest component of returns is clearly P/E repricing, followed by real earnings growth. Inflation and income returns are relatively stable through time. This observation implies that our real earnings growth and repricing forecasts are likely to be the least accurate and our inflation and income return forecasts are likely to be more accurate.

Mehra and Prescott (1985), and many others, argued that the equity premium of 4.5 percent was a multiple of the amount that should have been necessary to entice investors to hold on to the risky cash flows offered by equities instead of the certain cash flows offered by bonds. This contention spawned a huge literature on the "equity risk premium puzzle."[8] We have always been perplexed by a debate that suggests that investors were wrong while a specific macroeconomic theory is right, but Rajnish Mehra sheds additional light on this question elsewhere in this book.

---

[7]Because earnings were growing very quickly at the end of 2010, the more familiar P/E calculated as the current price divided by 12-month *forward* (forecast) earnings was lower than the P/E shown here.

[8]For surveys of this literature, see Kocherlakota (1996); Mehra (2003).

Looking to the Future

Next, we will examine each term in Equation 3 to determine which data are needed to forecast these terms over the moderately long run (10 years). Later in the paper, we will combine the elements to estimate, or forecast, the total return on the S&P 500 over that time frame. Finally, we will subtract the 10-year Treasury bond yield to arrive at the expected equity risk premium.

Income Return. The income return is the percentage of market capitalization that is distributed to shareholders in cash. Currently, companies have two principal means of distributing cash to shareholders: dividend payments and share repurchases. A third method, buying other companies for cash, "works" at the index level because index investors hold the acquired company and the acquiring company if the index is broad enough.

Until the mid-1980s, dividends were essentially the only means of distributing earnings. Since then, repurchases have skyrocketed in popularity, in part because they are a more tax-efficient means of distributing earnings and in part because companies with cash to distribute may not want to induce investors to expect a distribution every quarter (and cutting dividends is painful and often causes the stock price to decline). In addition, dividend-paying companies may suffer from a stigma of not being "growth" companies.

In fact, according to Grullon and Michaely (2000), the nominal growth rate of repurchases between 1980 and 1998 was 28.3 percent. Numerous other studies have shown that share repurchases have surpassed dividends as the preferred means of distributing earnings.[9] According to Fama and French (2001), only about one-fifth of publicly traded (nonfinancial and nonutility) companies paid any dividends at the time of their study, compared with about two-thirds as recently as 1978. So the "repurchase yield" now exceeds the dividend yield.

Currently (as of 18 March 2011), the dividend yield is 1.78 percent.[10] Like a bond yield, the current (not historical average) dividend yield is likely the best estimate of the income return over the near to intermediate future, so we use 1.78 percent as our estimate of D/P in Equation 3.

To estimate the repurchase yield, we used historical data over the longest period for which data were available from Standard & Poor's, the 12 years from 1998 through 2009. We calculated the annual repurchase yield as the sum of a given year's share repurchases divided by the end-of-year capitalization of the market. **Table 2** shows these data. The average of the 12 annual repurchase yields is 2.2 percent, which we use in our ERP estimate.

---

[9]See, for example, Fama and French (2001); Grullon and Michaely (2000); Fenn and Liang (2000).
[10]We obtained this number at www.multpl.com/s-p-500-dividend-yield on 18 March 2011.

Table 2. Repurchase Return of the S&P 500, 1998–2009

Year	Year-End Market Capitalization ($ billions)	Share Repurchases during Year ($ billions)	Share Repurchase Return (%)
1998	9,942.37	125	1.26
1999	12,314.99	142	1.15
2000	11,714.55	151	1.29
2001	10,463.39	132.21	1.26
2002	8,107.41	127.25	1.57
2003	10,285.83	131.05	1.27
2004	11,288.60	197.48	1.75
2005	11,254.54	349.22	3.10
2006	12,728.86	431.83	3.39
2007	12,867.85	589.12	4.58
2008	7,851.81	339.61	4.33
2009	9,927.56	137.60	1.39
Average			2.20

Source: Standard & Poor's.

It is possible to make the case for a much higher repurchase yield forecast by giving greater weight to more recent information (which is basically what we did with the dividend yield). According to Standard & Poor's (2008), "Over the past fourteen quarters, since the buyback boom began during the fourth quarter of 2004, S&P 500 issues have spent approximately $1.55 trillion on stock buybacks compared to . . . $783 billion on dividends." Although buybacks collapsed in 2009, they rebounded in 2010 and 2011. If the two-to-one ratio of buybacks to dividend payments observed by Standard & Poor's over 2004–2008 persists in the future, the repurchase yield will be as high as 3.5–3.6 percent. Aiming for a "fair and balanced" estimate, we use the lower number, 2.2 percent, which we obtained by weighting all 12 years of historical share repurchase data equally.[11]

We have not included cash buyouts in our estimate of the repurchase yield. From the perspective of an investor who holds an index containing companies A, B, C, and so forth, a cash buyout or takeover—a payment by company A to

---

[11]The use of this lower number is neutral, not conservative in the sense of numerically minimizing the ERP estimate. The reason is that there are offsetting biases. Our buyback estimate of 2.2 percent is too high because we do not subtract the historical contribution of buybacks to the dilution estimate (discussed later). And it is too low because very recent buyback rates have been much higher than 2.2 percent, not to mention the fact that we fully ignore the cash takeover yield.

an investor holding shares of company B in exchange for a tender of those shares—is no different from a share buyback, which is a payment by company A to an investor holding shares of A in exchange for a tender of *those* shares. Thus, the "cash buyout yield" needs to be added to the repurchase yield when summing all the pieces of $-\Delta S$. However, we do not have data for cash buyouts. If we did, they would increase our forecast of the equity risk premium (because cash buyouts must be a positive number and no other component of the ERP would change).

■ *Effect of Dilution on Income Return.* Dilution is the effect of new issuance of shares by existing companies and takes place through secondary offerings and the exercise of stock options. Dilution may be regarded as reflecting capital that needs to be injected from the labor market (or from elsewhere) into the stock market so investors can participate fully in the real economic growth described in the next section. Formally, dilution (expressed as an annual rate or a decrement to the total expected equity return) is the difference between the growth rate of dividends and the growth rate of dividends per share. If the payout ratio is assumed to be constant, dilution is also equal to the difference between the earnings growth rate and the EPS growth rate.

Grinold and Kroner (2002) estimated dilution from secondary offerings using historical data and dealt with stock options separately. Here, because we do not have the data to properly update the dilution estimates in Grinold and Kroner (2002), we use a shortcut: We directly adopt the 2 percent per year dilution estimate from Bernstein and Arnott (2003).

Bernstein and Arnott (2003) studied U.S. stocks from 1871 to 2000 and stocks from other countries over shorter periods. Instead of measuring the difference between the growth rate of earnings and that of EPS, they used a proxy: They measured the difference between the growth rate of total market capitalization and the capital appreciation return (price return) on existing shares. Dilution thus measured is net of share buybacks and cash buyouts (which are forms of negative dilution because giving cash back to shareholders is the opposite of raising capital by selling shares). The 2 percent dilution estimate for U.S. stocks is supported by evidence from other countries.[12]

---

[12]For a fuller discussion of dilution and an excellent description of the Bernstein and Arnott (2003) method, see Cornell (2010), who wrote, "Bernstein and Arnott (2003) suggested an ingenious procedure for estimating the combined impact of both effects [the need of existing corporations to issue new shares and the effect of start-ups] on the rate of growth of earnings to which current investors have a claim. They noted that total dilution on a marketwide basis can be measured by the ratio of the proportionate increase in market capitalization to the value-weighted proportionate increase in stock price. More precisely, net dilution for each period is given by the equation Net dilution = $(1 + c)/(1 + k) - 1$, where c is the percentage capitalization increase and k is the percentage increase in the value-weighted price index. Note that this dilution measure holds exactly only for the aggregate market portfolio" (p. 60).

We should subtract from the 2 percent dilution estimate that part of historical dilution that was due to buybacks and cash takeovers (but *not* the part of dilution that was due to stock option issuance because these cash flows went to employees, not shareholders). We do not have the data to perform these adjustments, however, so we do not attempt them. We simply use the 2 percent estimate. (Note that the number of buybacks was tiny until the mid-1980s—that is, over approximately the first 115 years of the 130-year sample—so historical buybacks probably had a minimal impact on the average rate of dilution for the entire period.)

▪ *Numerical Estimate of Income Return.* The income return forecast consists of the expected dividend yield, D/P, minus the expected rate of change in the number of shares outstanding, ΔS. The expected dividend yield is 1.78 percent. The number of new shares is expected to decline at a −0.2 percent annual rate, consisting of 2 percent dilution minus a 2.2 percent repurchase yield. After adding up all the pieces, the income return forecast is 1.98 percent.

Expected Real Earnings Growth. We expect real dividend growth, real earnings growth, and real GDP growth—all expressed in aggregate, not in per share or per capita, terms—to be equal to each other.

We expect dividend and earnings growth to be equal because we assume a constant payout ratio. Although the payout ratio has fluctuated widely in the past, it has trended downward over time, presumably because of tax and corporate liquidity considerations. But the decline has effectively stopped. **Figure 1** shows the dividend payout ratio for the U.S. stock market for 1900–2010; this curious series looks as though it has been bouncing between a declining lower bound (which has now leveled off near 30 percent) and an almost unlimited upper bound. The highest values of the payout ratio occurred when there was an earnings collapse (as in 2008–2009), but companies are loath to cut dividends more than they have to.[13] The lower bound reflects payout policy during normally prosperous times.

The current lower bound of about 30 percent would be a reasonable forecast of the payout ratio, but we do not need an explicit forecast because we have already assumed that it will be constant over the 10-year term of our ERP estimate. It is helpful to have empirical support for our assumption of a constant payout ratio, however, and the recent relative stability of the lower bound in Figure 1 provides this support.

---

[13]The all-time high level of the payout ratio, 397 percent, occurred in March 2009, when annualized monthly dividends per "share" of the S&P 500 were $27.25 and annualized monthly earnings per "share" were $6.86.

Figure 1. Payout Ratio of the U.S. Equity Market, 1900–2010

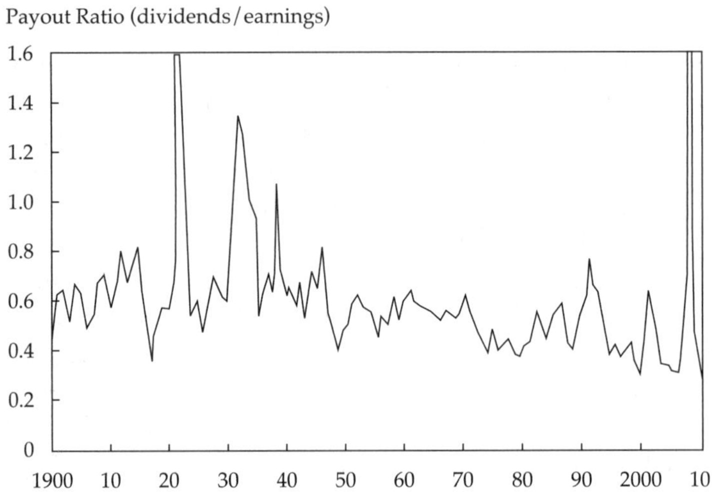

Source: Raw data are from Robert Shiller (www.econ.yale.edu/~shiller/data/ie_data.xls, as of 4 November 2011); calculations are by the authors.

We expect real earnings growth to equal real GDP growth for the macro-consistency reason stated earlier: Any other result would, in the very long run, lead to an absurdity—corporate profits either taking over national income entirely or disappearing. **Figure 2** shows the (trendless) fluctuations in the corporate profit share of GDP since 1947.

These observations leave us with the puzzle of forecasting real GDP growth. Grinold and Kroner (2002) engaged in a fairly typical macroeconomic analysis that involved productivity growth, labor force growth, and the expected difference between S&P 500 earnings and overall corporate profits. They did not use historical averages or trends directly as forecasts; rather, they argued that the data plus other factors justified the conclusion that real GDP would most likely grow at 3 percent over the relevant forecast period and that real S&P 500 earnings would grow at 3.5 percent.

Real economic growth, by definition, equals real productivity growth plus labor force growth. Although we can update the historical productivity and labor force growth numbers, doing so would not produce an especially useful forecast any more than it did for Grinold and Kroner (2002), who distanced themselves somewhat from the productivity and labor force growth approach. The reason is that extrapolating recent trends in these components of economic growth can produce unrealistically high or low expectations, and using

Figure 2. Quarterly U.S. Corporate Profits as a Percentage of GDP, 1947–2010

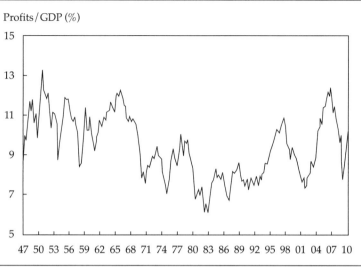

Note: Profits are pre-tax.

Source: Haver Analytics, citing U.S. National Income and Product Accounts data.

historical averages provides no insight into possible future changes in the components, which are important. Nevertheless, updates of these components are provided for informational purposes in **Figure 3**.

We can, however, use a different decomposition of real economic growth, which is also definitional: Expected GDP growth equals expected *per capita* GDP growth plus expected population growth. We believe that population growth is easier to forecast than labor force growth because the latter is partly endogenous (e.g., people work longer if they need the money because of a weak economy).[14]

Figure 4 shows that since 1789, real per capita U.S. GDP has grown at a fairly constant 1.8 percent compound annual rate. Cornell (2010) arrived at a global estimate from the high-growth postwar period (1960–2006) that is higher, but not dramatically so: 2.42 percent for mature economies and 2.79 percent for emerging economies. A cautious forecast is that the 1.8 percent growth rate will continue. If this forecast entails substantial risk, it is to the upside because an investment in the S&P 500 is not a pure bet on the U.S. economy; many, if not most, of the companies in the index are global companies that sell to markets that are growing more rapidly than the U.S. market.

[14]Population growth is also partly endogenous (because the decisions of how many children to have, whether to emigrate, and so forth, may depend on economic performance). These effects, however, operate with long lags and tend to move the population growth rate slowly.

Figure 3. U.S. Real Productivity and Labor Force Growth Rates, 1971–2009

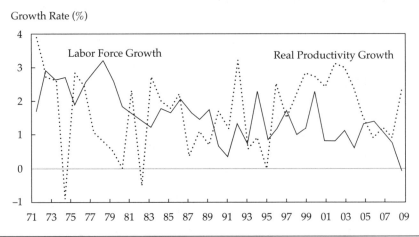

Source: Organisation for Economic Co-Operation and Development, OECD StatExtracts (http://stats.oecd.org/Index.aspx, as of 14 November 2011: total labour force, U.S., and labour productivity annual growth rate, U.S.).

Figure 4. Real U.S. GDP per Capita, 1789–2008

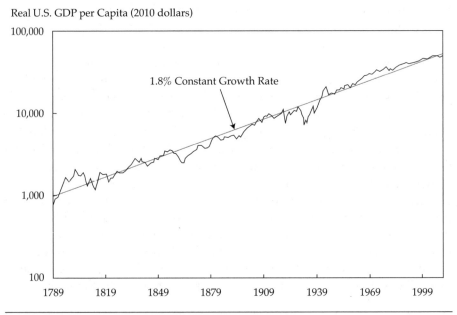

Source: Data are from Robert D. Arnott.

©2011 The Research Foundation of CFA Institute

We add to the 1.8 percent real per capita GDP growth estimate the Economist Intelligence Unit 10-year U.S. population growth estimate of 0.85 percent,[15] which gives a total real GDP growth forecast of 2.65 percent. This number is slightly below current consensus estimates.

This simplified method presents some difficulty because if the rate of dilution is 2 percent at all population growth rates, then population growth has a one-for-one effect on the estimate of the expected return on equities and, therefore, on the ERP. This suggests an easy beat-the-market strategy: Invest only in countries with the fastest population growth. This strategy has not worked well in the past, and even if it did over some sample period, easy beat-the-market strategies are usually illusory. Thus, the dilution estimate should probably be higher for countries with high population growth rates or for a country during periods of above-normal population growth. Although the logic of using a link to real GDP growth to forecast the stock market has great intuitive appeal, putting it into practice with any precision will take more work and more thought regarding dilution.[16]

Expected Inflation. Because we are deriving the ERP relative to Treasury bonds, we do not need our own inflation forecast as much as we need an estimate of the inflation rate that is priced into the 10-year Treasury bond market. Historical inflation rates have no bearing on this number, so we do not present them. Fortunately, the yield spread between 10-year nominal Treasury bonds and 10-year TIPS is a direct, although volatile, measure of the inflation rate that is expected by bondholders. (The spread also includes an inflation risk premium, present in nominal bond yields but not in TIPS yields, for which we need to adjust.)

---

[15]This number was obtained at http://7marketspot.com/archives/2276 on 2 May 2011 under the heading "USA economy: Ten-year growth outlook" in the column "2011–20." If we instead used real productivity growth plus labor force growth to estimate real GDP growth, we would get a slightly higher number for real productivity growth and a slightly lower number for labor force growth, which would provide a very similar overall real GDP forecast.

[16]Our simplified method has some other characteristics worth noting. It does not specifically account for the wedge between population growth and labor force growth if the proportion of retirees (or children) in the population is expected to change. A growing unproductive retiree population should be considered bearish. Many would-be retirees, however, are not financially prepared for retirement, and, willingly or not, will work longer than they originally anticipated, which contributes to GDP. In addition, in an advanced technological society, an aging population distribution within the workforce is not all bad! We are accustomed to thinking of young workers as productive and older workers as unproductive, but this is the case only in a fairly primitive economy where the primary job description is something like "lift this and put it over there." In a technological society, young workers are unproductive—often startlingly so, earning only the minimum wage—and older workers produce most of the added value and make the lion's share of the money. Nevertheless, young workers' productivity grows quickly and older workers' productivity grows slowly or shrinks, so the impact of an aging workforce on *rates of change* in productivity may be less salutary than the impact on the *level* of productivity.

On 22 April 2011, the breakeven inflation rate (the yield spread described above) was 2.60 percent.[17] This rate is high by recent standards—it was as low as 1.5 percent in September 2010—but it is typical of the longer history of the series. Recent concerns about very high and rapidly growing levels of public indebtedness (of the U.S. government, of local governments in the United States, and of non-U.S. governments) have contributed to the increase in inflation expectations. We subtract 0.2 percent for the inflation risk premium to arrive at a 2.4 percent compound annual inflation forecast over the next 10 years.[18]

Expected Repricing. Grinold and Kroner (2002, p. 15, Chart 8) conducted an analysis of the market's P/E that led them to include a nonzero (–0.75 percent per year) value for the repricing term, ΔPE, in Equation 3. At the time the analysis was conducted (November 2001), the market's conventional trailing P/E (price divided by one-year trailing earnings) was a lofty 29.7 and the "Shiller P/E" (price divided by 10-year trailing real earnings) was 30.0, which prompted the authors to conclude that the P/E was likely to decline.[19] (The Shiller P/E is designed to smooth out fluctuations caused by yearly changes in earnings.) And decline it did.

Today, the situation is different. **Figure 5** shows the conventional P/E and the Shiller P/E of the U.S. market. Today's conventional P/E of 18.5 is only modestly higher than the very long-run (1900–2010) average P/E of 15.7, and it is lower than the more recent long-run (1970–2010) average P/E of 18.9. The Shiller P/E tells a slightly less favorable story: The current value is 22.4, compared with an average of 16.3 over 1900–2010 and 19.2 over 1970–2010.[20] Because it averages 10 years of trailing earnings, however, the current Shiller P/E includes an earnings collapse in 2008–2009 that is almost literally unprecedented; even the Great Depression did not see as sharp a contraction in S&P composite index earnings, although overall corporate profits in 1932 were negative. (Huge losses in a few large companies, such as those that occurred in 2008–2009, go a long way toward erasing the profits of other companies when summed across an index.) Only the depression of 1920–1921 is comparable.

Thus, we see no justification for using a nonzero value for the repricing term in Equation 3. The market's current level is already reflected in the (low) dividend yield. To include a repricing term even though the dividend yield already incorporates the market's valuation is, theoretically, not double-counting because the influence of the dividend yield is amortized over an infinite horizon,

---

[17] See www.bloomberg.com/apps/quote?ticker=USGGBE10:IND.

[18] This estimate of the inflation risk premium comes from Hördahl (2008, p. 31, Graph 2).

[19] Shiller (2000) describes the Shiller P/E.

[20] In this section, "current" values are as of December 2010.

Figure 5. Conventional and Shiller P/Es for the U.S. Equity Market, 1900–2010

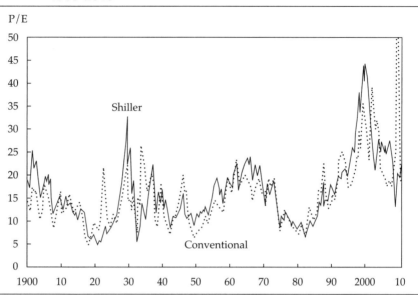

Note: The October 2009 conventional P/E equals 86.

Source: Spreadsheet available at Robert Shiller's website (www.econ.yale.edu/~shiller/data/ie_data.xls).

whereas our forecast is for only the next 10 years. Thus, if we believe that the market is mispriced in such a way that it will be fully corrected within 10 years, a nonzero repricing term is warranted. Although Grinold and Kroner (2002) argued that the market P/E was too high at that time and would decline at an expected rate of 0.75 percent per year over the forecast horizon, we think the market is currently not too high (or too low), and our repricing forecast is zero.

Bringing It All Together

In this section, we estimate the expected total nominal return on equities, as expressed in Equation 3, using the inputs we derived in the foregoing sections. We then subtract the 10-year nominal Treasury bond yield to arrive at our estimate of the ERP over the next 10 years.

$$\text{Income return } (D/P - \Delta S) = 1.78 \text{ percent dividend yield}$$
$$- (-0.2 \text{ percent repurchase yield net of dilution})$$
$$= 1.98 \text{ percent.}$$

$$\text{Capital gain } (i + g + \Delta PE) = 2.4 \text{ percent inflation}$$
$$+ 1.8 \text{ percent real per capita GDP growth}$$
$$+ 0.85 \text{ percent population growth}$$
$$= 5.05 \text{ percent.}$$

Total expected equity return = 1.98 percent + 5.05 percent
= 7.03 percent (rounded to 7 percent)
− 3.40 percent 10-year Treasury bond
on 22 April 2011[21]
= 3.6 percent expected ERP over 10-year Treasuries.

Arithmetic vs. Geometric Mean Forecasts

Our forecasts thus far have been geometric means (r_G). To estimate the equivalent arithmetic mean return expectation (r_A) for use as an optimizer input, we rely on the following approximation:

$$1 + r_G \approx (1 + r_A) - \frac{\sigma^2}{2}. \qquad (4)$$

We use standard deviations drawn from 1970 to 2010 because we do not necessarily expect bond returns to be as placid as they have been recently. Thus, for the purpose of estimating standard deviations, we include this long period because it includes the bond bear market of 1970–1980 and the dramatic subsequent recovery.[22] We obtain the following:

Expected arithmetic mean equity total return = 8.59 percent.

Expected arithmetic mean 10-year Treasury bond total return = 3.96 percent.

Difference (expected arithmetic mean ERP) = 4.63 percent.

A limitation of this study is that we use U.S., not global, macroeconomic data in our estimate of the expected return on the S&P 500. The S&P 500 is a global index, in that it contains many companies that earn most, or a substantial share, of their profits outside the United States. Perhaps global economic growth rates are more relevant to the expected return on the S&P 500 than U.S. growth rates. Future research should examine this possibility.

Assessing the Previous Grinold and Kroner Forecast

Grinold and Kroner (2002) identified three camps of ERP forecasters: "risk premium is dead," "rational exuberance," and "risk is rewarded." They called the first two views "extreme" and wished to be counted among the moderate "risk is rewarded" camp, in keeping with the belief that markets are generally efficient and that prices, therefore, do not stray far from genuine values for very long.

---

[21]This number was obtained from Yahoo! Finance on 22 April 2011.
[22]Stocks = 17.68 percent; bonds = 9.73 percent (these data are from Aswath Damodaran's website, http://pages.stern.nyu.edu/~adamodar, as of 3 June 2011).

Grinold and Kroner's (2002) forecast, evaluated over 2002–2011, was too high. The main problem was the volatile repricing term. They seriously underestimated the speed with which the unusually high P/Es that then prevailed would revert toward their historical mean. In this paper, we forecast a repricing of zero, consistent with our view that the market is finally, after two bear markets and two recoveries, roughly fairly priced. Because the repricing term is noisy, we know that our current forecast is more likely to be too high or too low than just right when evaluated over the next 10 years. We believe, however, that we have identified the middle of the range of likely outcomes. Although black swans, fat tails, and tsunamis are the talk of the day, such large unexpected events tend to fade in importance as they are averaged in with less dramatic events over extended periods and the underlying long-term trends reveal themselves once more.[23] We expect moderate growth in the stock market.

The authors thank Antti Ilmanen for his very generous contribution of a number of different data sources and for his wise counsel. Paul Kaplan also provided helpful advice and contributed invaluable data.

REFERENCES

Arnott, Robert D., and Ronald J. Ryan. 2001. "The Death of the Risk Premium." *Journal of Portfolio Management*, vol. 27, no. 3 (Spring):61–74.

Bernstein, William J., and Robert D. Arnott. 2003. "Earnings Growth: The Two Percent Dilution." *Financial Analysts Journal*, vol. 59, no. 5 (September/October):47–55.

Cornell, Bradford. 2010. "Economic Growth and Equity Investing." *Financial Analysts Journal*, vol. 66, no. 1 (January/February):54–64.

Diermeier, Jeffrey J., Roger G. Ibbotson, and Laurence B. Siegel. 1984. "The Supply of Capital Market Returns." *Financial Analysts Journal*, vol. 40, no. 2 (March/April):74–80.

Fama, Eugene F., and Kenneth R. French. 2001. "Disappearing Dividends: Changing Firm Characteristics or Lower Propensity to Pay?" *Journal of Financial Economics*, vol. 60, no. 1 (April):3–43.

Fenn, George W., and Nellie Liang. 2000. "Corporate Payout Policy and Managerial Stock Incentives." Working paper, Federal Reserve Board (March).

Grinold, Richard C., and Kenneth F. Kroner. 2002. "The Equity Risk Premium: Analyzing the Long-Run Prospects for the Stock Market." *Investment Insights*, vol. 5, no. 3 (July):7–33.

---

[23] Siegel (2010) provided a skeptical look at the phenomenon of black swans.

Grullon, Gustavo, and Roni Michaely. 2000. "Dividends, Share Repurchases and the Substitution Hypothesis." Unpublished manuscript, Johnson Graduate School of Management, Cornell University (April).

Hördahl, Peter. 2008. "The Inflation Risk Premium in the Term Structure of Interest Rates." *BIS Quarterly Review* (September):23–38.

Ibbotson, Roger G., and Peng Chen. 2003. "Long-Run Stock Returns: Participating in the Real Economy." *Financial Analysts Journal*, vol. 59, no. 1 (January/February):88–98.

Ibbotson SBBI. 2011. *2011 Classic Yearbook: Market Results for Stocks, Bonds, Bills, and Inflation, 1926–2010* (Chicago: Morningstar).

Kaplan, Paul D. 2011. *Frontiers of Modern Asset Allocation*. Hoboken, NJ: John Wiley & Sons.

Kocherlakota, Narayana R. 1996. "The Equity Premium: It's Still a Puzzle." *Journal of Economic Literature*, vol. 34, no. 1 (March):42–71.

Mehra, Rajnish. 2003. "The Equity Premium: Why Is It a Puzzle?" *Financial Analysts Journal*, vol. 59, no. 1 (January/February):54–69.

Mehra, Rajnish, and Edward C. Prescott. 1985. "The Equity Premium: A Puzzle." *Journal of Monetary Economics*, vol. 15, no. 2 (March):145–161.

Shiller, Robert J. 2000. *Irrational Exuberance*. 2nd ed. Princeton, NJ: Princeton University Press.

Siegel, Laurence B. 2010. "Black Swan or Black Turkey? The State of Economic Knowledge and the Crash of 2007–2009." *Financial Analysts Journal*, vol. 66, no. 4 (July/August):6–10.

Standard & Poor's. 2008. "S&P 500 Stock Buybacks Retreat in Q1 but Remain Strong." Press release (18 June).

Equity Risk Premium Myths

Robert D. Arnott
Chair and Founder, Research Affiliates, LLC

For the capital markets to "work," stocks should produce higher returns than bonds. Otherwise, stockholders would not be paid for the additional risk they take for being lower down in the capital structure. This relationship should be particularly true when stocks are compared with government bonds that (ostensibly) cannot default. It comes as no surprise, therefore, that stockholders have enjoyed outsized returns from their investments. When investors collectively expect an outsized return, as they should relative to bonds or cash, we call this expectation the "equity risk premium."

Many of the controversies surrounding the equity risk premium (ERP) are rooted in semantics: The same term is used for multiple purposes. The ERP may be based on the difference between two backward-looking rates of return—which is *not* a risk premium because it reflects past returns rather than return expectations—or on forward-looking return expectations. It may be based on single-year arithmetic return differences or compounded multiyear geometric return differences. It may be based on comparisons with cash or with bonds or with U.S. Treasury Inflation-Protected Securities (TIPS).

In any dialogue on the topic, these semantic differences mean that we may, unfortunately, be talking past one another. A 1 percent ERP (calculated as an expected multiyear geometric return difference between stocks and bonds) can be consistent with a 7 percent ERP (calculated as an expected single-year arithmetic return difference between stocks and cash at a time when the yield curve is steep, as it is at this writing), and both can be wholly consistent with a 6.5 percent observed historical excess return (the arithmetic average single-year difference between stock and cash returns over the past 60 years, which many observers erroneously label the "equity risk premium").[1]

So, perhaps this discussion should begin with definitions—the distinction between excess returns and the ERP. Because cash yields are inherently short term and hugely variable whereas forward-looking stock market returns are inherently long term and rather more stable (the sum of the yield and long-term expected growth in income is not likely to move more than 1–2 percentage points in a single year), I prefer to compare expected stock market returns with the return expectations for forward-looking government bonds or TIPS.

---

[1] By convention, I express the equity risk premium as a "percentage" rather than the more accurate "percentage points" or in basis points.

Backward-looking excess returns are hugely variable. Over rolling 20-year spans, the gap between stock and bond market returns—the excess return for stocks—ranges from +20.7 percent to −10.1 percent per year. Wow! Most of us would consider 20 years to be a long time span. Yet, few observers would consider a 20 percent annual risk premium to be reasonable; none would consider a −10 percent risk premium reasonable.

These historical excess returns also exhibit large negative serial correlation with subsequent excess returns. Over the past 210 years, the correlation between consecutive 10-year stock market excess returns over 10-year government bonds has been a whopping −38 percent. When stocks beat bonds by a wide margin in one decade, they reversed with reasonable reliability over the next decade. This correlation is both statistically significant and economically meaningful.

Forecasting the future ERP by extrapolating past excess returns is, therefore, fraught with peril. Yet, extrapolating the past is so tempting that much of the finance community sets return expectations in exactly this fashion. No wonder our industry got it so wrong at the peak of the technology bubble in 2000: The average corporate pension fund was using an all-time-high 9.5 percent "pension return assumption" for conventional balanced 60 percent equity/40 percent bond portfolios at a time when bond yields were 6 percent and the stock market offered an all-time-low 1.1 percent dividend yield! There may also be a Machiavellian aspect to this "expectation," in that some pension plan sponsors may have known the forecasts were too high but used them anyway to avoid having to increase contributions to their pension plans.

Except when I specifically indicate to the contrary, I use the term "excess returns" to refer to realized differences between stock market returns and long-term government bond returns and the term "the ERP" to refer to expected (forward-looking) long-term differences between stock returns and long bond market expected returns (geometric or compounded annual rates). Occasionally, I use cash or long-term TIPS rather than long-term government bonds, but when I do, I acknowledge that I am doing so.

Myths

Over the years, a number of myths related to the ERP have emerged. One of the most widely "cited" myths is that the ERP is 5 percent. Before discussing the natural limits for the risk premium, I will explore an array of these ERP myths and reflect on why we so eagerly embrace myths rather than test them to objectively gauge their legitimacy.

Take, for example, the myth that the ERP is a static 5 percent. According to Ibbotson Associates (now Morningstar) data, equity investors earned a real return of 8 percent and stocks outpaced bonds by more than 5 percent from

1926 until the early 2000s.[2] More recently, these figures have sagged to 6.5 percent and 4.5 percent, respectively. Intuition suggests that investors should not require such outsized returns in order to bear equity market risk. If we examine the historical record, neither the 8 percent real return nor the 5 percent risk premium for stocks relative to government bonds has ever been a realistic *expectation*, except at major market bottoms or at times of crisis, such as wartime.

Should investors have expected these returns in the past, and why shouldn't they continue to do so? We can break this question into two parts. First, can we derive an objective estimate of what investors had good reasons to expect in the past? Second, should we expect less in the future than we have earned in the past, and if so, why?

The answers to these questions lie in the difference between the observed excess return and the prospective risk premium. When we distinguish between past excess returns and future expected risk premiums, the idea that future risk premiums should be different from past excess returns is entirely reasonable.

Most of the ERP myths take on the character of a classic urban legend— so seductively plausible that they linger despite overwhelming evidence to the contrary. Note that most of these myths can be used to rationalize a higher, not a lower, ERP. No one seems to construct a myth or a fable to explain why we should expect lower returns!

The myths I examine include the following:

- *The risk premium is 5 percent and changes little, except perhaps in proportion to a stock's beta.* Nothing in finance theory requires any such assumption, but the notion of a large risk premium has been used to justify some truly heroic growth assumptions when yields or payout ratios have been low.

- *The ERP is static over time, across markets, and across companies.* Higher or lower yields, yield spreads, valuation multiples, and so forth have no bearing on the ERP. The proponents of this myth argue that constantly changing yields, spreads, and valuation multiples reflect changing investor expectations for future growth—in a fashion that offsets the yield, spread, or valuation changes—leaving the ERP unaltered. Nothing in neoclassical finance theory, however, suggests that the ERP must be static. Moreover, behavioral finance observers would emphatically contradict the notion of a static ERP because risk, risk expectations, and risk tolerance are all nonstatic.

- *The "ERP Puzzle": Stocks beat bonds by more than they should.* If we adhere to the view that the excess return for stocks should be measured in 10ths of a percent (10s of basis points), as most utility functions suggest for the long-term investor, this observation is true. But the ERP Puzzle seems to

---

[2]This section is excerpted and amended from Arnott and Bernstein (2002).

be posed as though 5 percent is the excess return that needs to be explained. Such a high excess return has not been earned in "normal" markets. In the absence of gains in valuation multiples, an excess return of 2–3 percent is more normal, and even that margin seems to be more consistent with high yields than with the low yields we observe today.

- *Stocks will beat bonds for anyone willing to think long term, which is typically taken to mean 20–30 years or longer.* This myth lingers in spite of a 41-year span (early 1968 to early 2009) in which the returns of ordinary long U.S. T-bonds eclipsed the S&P 500 Index return. Non-U.S. examples counter to this myth also abound.

- *When yields and payout ratios are low, stock buybacks can replace the dividend in a tax-advantaged fashion.* However, true buybacks—that is, buybacks that truly reduce shares outstanding rather than merely recapture shares issued in a context of management stock option redemption—are much more the exception than the rule.

- *Stock market earnings grow with GDP.* If this myth were true, the expected return on stocks would match yield plus expected GDP growth. Unfortunately, this enduring myth ignores the fact that the share of corporate profits in GDP growth consists of the growth in existing enterprises *plus* the creation of new enterprises. The "new enterprises" portion is often the larger component of real GDP growth. Therefore, the ERP is much smaller than adherents to this misconception expect.

- *Dividends do not really matter.* This myth is twofold. First, it involves the belief that *lower yields are entirely consistent with continued high return and a high ERP.* In an efficient market, investors will accept a lower yield whenever they are confident that future real growth in earnings will make up the difference. But overwhelming global evidence suggests a strong positive link between the dividend yield and both the subsequent real return for stocks and the subsequent excess return of stocks over bonds.

  The second part of this myth is that *lower payout ratios lead to faster earnings growth.* The Modigliani and Miller indifference theorem is often used to justify this view. But M&M is a theory based on a large array of simplifying assumptions and, therefore, an approximation of reality.

Both of these instances show that, in reality, dividends *do* matter.

The 5 Percent Risk Premium

Ibbotson Associates—whose annual data compendium covers U.S. stocks, T-bonds, and T-bills since January 1926—shows the S&P 500 compounding through February 2011 at an annual rate of 9.8 percent, versus 5.5 percent for long-term government bonds, which is an excess return of 4.3 percent. This return compounds exponentially with time. Albert Einstein whimsically declared that compound interest is "the most powerful force in the universe." Disregarding inflation, taxes, transaction costs, and fees, a $1,000 U.S. stock investment in 1926 would have ballooned to $3 million by February 2011, versus $94,000 for an investment in long-term bonds—a 32-fold difference.

In the 1980s and 1990s, stocks—bolstered by soaring valuation multiples—compounded at, respectively, 17.6 percent and 18.2 percent per year. As a result, "Stocks for the Long Run" became the mantra for long-term investing, as well as the title of a best-selling book by Siegel (2007). This view is now embedded into the psyche of an entire generation of professional and casual investors, who ignore the fact that much of that outsized return in the 1980s and 1990s was a consequence of soaring valuation multiples and tumbling yields. Because most investors anchor their decisions on personal experience, we have a population that largely assumes that this long-term 5 percent excess return of stocks over bonds is their birthright. This view constitutes the "cult of equities."

Let's Talk Really Long Term. For those willing to do the homework, very long-term stock and bond data exist for the United States. The picture of the difference between stocks and bonds if we start at 1802 is not quite as rosy as it is from 1926 to 2010; therefore, this view does not receive as much attention from the relentlessly optimistic stock sellers of Wall Street. From 1802 to 2010, U.S. stocks generated a 7.9 percent annual return, versus 5.1 percent for long-term government bonds. So, the realized excess return was cut to 2.8 percent—a one-third reduction—by including an additional 125 years of capital market history.

Of course, many observers declare 19th century data irrelevant. A lot has changed. The survival of the United States as we know it was in doubt during the first part of the century (the War of 1812), and in the middle stages, we waged a debilitating civil war. Government bonds were thus not riskless. And by modern standards, the United States was an emerging market. Citizens lived shorter lives than now, and the economy was notably short on global trade and long on subsistence agriculture. Furthermore, three major wars and four depressions—two roughly comparable to the Great Depression—occurred between 1800 and 1870, a span during which the data on market returns are notably meager.

One could as easily make the case, however, that the 20th century is not representative either. The 20th century brought great and unexpected fortune to the United States and its equity markets. The country was not invaded and occupied by a foreign power, and it did not suffer a government overthrow. For contrast, consider the return on capital for Russian investors after the Bolshevik Revolution—a 100 percent loss. Benjamin Graham cautioned on the difference between the loss *on* capital (a drop in price, from which the investor can recover) and a loss *of* capital (100 percent loss, from which the investor cannot recover). Russia's stock market was not alone in devastating losses of capital in the 20th century; 2 additional markets of the top 15 in 1900, Egypt and China, suffered a 100 percent loss of capital; Argentina, Germany (twice), and Japan (once) came close.

Markets tend to be unkind to those who ignore history, and the severity of the penalty is highly correlated with our reliance on viewing a span of history that is too short. The long history of the markets should not be ignored even when we are dealing with the shorter time horizons of most investment programs. Even for such "perpetual" institutions as university endowments, the relevant horizon is only 10–30 years. As Bernstein (1997) commented about 80–100 years of data, ". . . this kind of long run will exceed the life expectancies of most people mature enough to be invited to join such boards of trustees" (p. 22).

Nonetheless, the relevant investment span should be long enough that equity investors will be rewarded for bearing risk, right? Not always! As displayed in **Table 1**, trailing returns for stocks have not come close to the excess returns over bonds that we have all come to expect, even after stocks worldwide doubled from the lows reached during the global financial crisis that began in early March 2009. They have not come close in the United States, in the rest of the developed world, and most assuredly not in the emerging markets.

Where is the wealth creation implied by the long-term Ibbotson data? Stock market investors took the risk. They rode out every bubble, every crash, every spectacular bankruptcy and bear market during a 30-year stretch that finished with a 100 percent gain in two years. How much was their cumulative excess return for the blood, sweat, and tears spilled with all this volatility? Through 2010—a splendid span for bonds as yields tumbled for 30 years while

Table 1. Annualized Returns for Stocks over the "Long Run," for 10, 20, and 30 Years Ended 2010: Where Is the Reward?

	10-Year Return	20-Year Return	30-Year Return
S&P 500	1.41%	9.14%	10.71%
Ibbotson U.S. long-term government bonds	6.64	8.44	10.18
U.S. equity risk premium	−5.23	0.70	0.53
MSCI Europe/Australasia/Far East Index (net)	3.50	5.85	
JPM Government Bond Index: Global ex U.S. TR USD[a]	7.64	7.07	
International equity risk premium	−4.14	−1.22	

[a]TR stands for "total return."

Source: Based on data from Morningstar EnCorr.

©2011 The Research Foundation of CFA Institute

stock market yields followed a less relentless downward course—the cumulative excess return was only 0.66 percent per year. Indeed, investors who incurred the ups and downs over the past 10 years have lost money compared with what they could have earned from long-term government bonds. They have paid for the privilege of incurring stomach-churning risk. Not only did T-bond investors sleep better and more over the past 10 years than stock investors, but they also ate better.

Although recent years have been far from normal, a 30-year stock market excess return of approximately zero is a slap in the face for the legions of "stocks at any price" long-term investors. Yet, it is not the first extended drought. From 1803 to 1857, U.S. equities struggled; the stock investor would have received a third of the ending wealth of the bond investor. For the 1803 investor in U.S. stocks, the shortfall against the bond investor was only recovered in 1871. These early U.S. stock market return data are of dubious quality, but the better U.K. data show a similar trajectory. Most observers would be shocked to learn a 68-year stretch of stock market underperformance occurred in either country. After a 72-year run from 1857 through 1929, when stocks outperformed handily in both the United States and the United Kingdom, another dry spell ensued. From 1929 through 1949, U.S. stocks failed to match bonds. It is the only long-term shortfall in the Ibbotson time sample until the 40-year period ending in March 2009. Perhaps the spectacular 1950–99 aftermath of the extraordinary period of history comprising the Great Depression and World War II lulled recent investors into a false sense of security regarding extended equity performance.

The Odds. Fortunately for the capital markets and equity investors, an examination of history shows that stocks have a high tendency to outperform government bonds over 10- and 20-year periods. **Figure 1** illustrates rolling 10- and 20-year "win rates" for equities versus government bonds for Ibbotson data and data for the whole 1802–2010 period. The Ibbotson time frame confirms investor behavior in the 30 years since Ibbotson and Sinquefield published their groundbreaking study (1977). For the vast majority of periods—92 percent for 10 years and almost 98 percent for 20 years—equities outperformed bonds. The solid consistency goes hand-in-hand with a large average excess return; stocks beat long government bonds by 4.6 percent per year over this span. But the longer-term data are much less convincing than the Ibbotson data. Equities outperformed in 70 percent of the 10-year periods and 84 percent of the 20-year spans, which is wholly consistent with the smaller 2.7 percent risk premium earned by stocks over long bonds during this much longer two-century span. Similar data for other countries indicate that the advantage of equities is even less reliable there than in the United States.

Figure 1. Percentage of Time U.S. Stocks Have Outperformed Long-Term U.S. Government Bonds over Monthly Rolling Periods

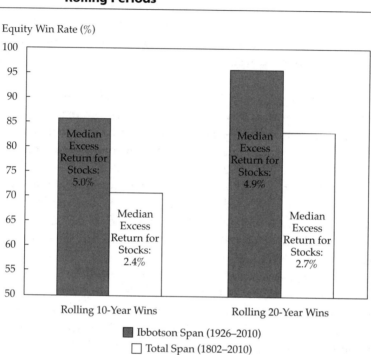

Odds are still with the equity investor. Odds of 70 percent or 80 percent are pretty good. In professional basketball, those odds would be average to above-average free throw percentages. But the relatively small probability of failure masks the magnitude of a miss. Just as a single missed free throw can cost a basketball championship, so too can an equity "miss" lead to drastic consequences, as the past 10 years have shown. Superior equity returns are not guaranteed, so why does our industry act as if they are? More importantly, why do investors take all that risk for a skinny equity premium?

We at Research Affiliates do not expect bonds to beat stocks over the next 10 or 20 years. I offer this brief history lesson to illuminate the fact that the much vaunted 4–5 percent risk premium for holding stocks is unreliable and a dangerous assumption to rely on for future plans. In our view, a more reasonable assumption would be 2–3 percent, which reflects history excluding the rise in valuation multiples of the past 30 years. A consideration of today's low starting yields, the prospective challenges from our addiction to debt-financed consumption, and headwinds from demographics would put the ERP closer to 1 percent.

To act as if the past 200 years were fully representative of the future would be foolish. For one thing, the United States was an emerging market for much of that period, with only a handful of industries and an unstable currency. In the past century, we dodged challenges and difficulties that laid waste to the plans of investors in many countries. Taleb (2007) has pointed out that black swans—unwelcome outliers that spring up well beyond the bounds of normalcy—are a recurring phenomenon; the abnormal is, indeed, normal. U.S. stock market history is but a single sample of a large and unknowable population of potential outcomes.

Peter Bernstein relentlessly reminded us that there are things we can never know, that prosperity and investing success are inherently "risky" and can disappear in a flash. Uncertainty is always with us; the old adage puts it succinctly: If you want God to laugh, tell him your plans. Concentrating the majority of one's investment portfolio in one investment category on the basis of an unknowable and fickle long-term equity premium is a dangerous game of "probability chicken."

The Unchanging ERP

An enduring myth is the notion that the ERP should be static across time and across assets. Why, however, should British Petroleum, struggling to recover from the largest oil spill in history, command the same risk premium as Apple, enjoying acclaim for a product line that serves the appetites of the consumer market with remarkable prescience? BP seems to be riskier than Apple. Should it not command a higher risk premium (and, therefore, a lower price)? Why should the broad stock market command the same risk premium when it is gripped by fear of the apocalypse in the financial services community (as in early 2009) as when optimism is being fueled by a booming economy and a startling surge in technological innovation (as in early 2000)? The year 2009 felt riskier than 2000. So, should stocks have broadly commanded a higher risk premium (and, therefore, a lower price) in 2009 than in 2000? Intuitively, the ERP should obviously vary both across time and across assets.

Many in academia like the simplicity of a fixed risk premium. Simplicity is a good thing, but recall that Einstein was fond of saying, "Make everything as simple as possible, but not simpler." A fixed risk premium is a hypothesis, not a fact; indeed, it is one of the least defensible hypotheses in the finance world today. There is no reason to assume a static risk premium. Nothing in neoclassical finance theory requires a static risk premium, and behavioral finance essentially insists on a risk premium that varies over time and across assets. Indeed, recent developments in neoclassical finance theory have focused on time-varying and cross-sectional differences in risk premiums.[3]

A question that emerges from these recent developments in neoclassical finance is: What's the difference between an inefficient market and a market in which the risk premium varies both cross-sectionally and across time? Would it not be easier to simply dispense with the efficient market hypothesis and recognize that price equals an invisible fair value plus or minus a mean-reverting error? Siegel (2006) and Hirshleifer, Glazer, and Hirshleifer (2005) have both likened the debate about this question to the slow acceptance of Copernican cosmology in preference to the bizarre epicycles that were needed to defend Aristotle for more than 1,500 years. Without Copernicus, people could explain the movement of the planets with considerable precision, but because the basic pre-Copernican theory was wrong, no one could figure out why. With Copernicus, Newton was able to answer "why."

The notion that fair value equals price deprives fair value of any independent meaning. Moreover, this notion deprives the academic, empirical, and practitioner communities of a rich opportunity to consider the mathematics and the practical implications of a world in which price and value differ.

The ERP Puzzle: Less Puzzling Than We Might Think

Academia has been abuzz for most of three decades about the ERP Puzzle: Stocks have delivered premium returns relative to bonds or cash that are outsized relative to the return premium that would, in theory, suffice to justify the incremental risk. Although much of macroeconomics points toward a *rational* ERP (for stocks relative to bonds) measured in 10ths of a percent, observed excess returns over long spans have often been 5 percent or more. Until recently.

An observed excess return of 5 percent is not the same thing as an *ex ante* expectation for a 5 percent ERP. For example, if stock market valuation multiples soar, adding a large unexpected increment to returns, excess returns can soundly exceed the *ex ante* ERP. But the opposite can happen just as readily. Indeed, the opposite was the nature of the past decade: Stock market yields nearly doubled as bond yields tumbled, fueling both the bleak stock market returns and the robust real returns for bonds. Yet, despite stocks delivering 700 bps less than long-term

---

[3]The capital asset pricing model allowed for cross-sectional differences in expected returns, but these returns were driven solely by beta. Many extra dimensions seem to be necessary to fit the data; Fama and French (1992, 1993) explored the joint influence of size and valuation, but a myriad of other dimensions have appeared in recent years. Campbell and Shiller (1988) opened the door in the 1980s for time-varying stock market returns; this approach was subsequently extended by Fama and French (1988). Theoretical explanations were explored by Campbell and Cochrane (1999). Finally, Cochrane's (2011) presidential address to the American Finance Association focuses specifically on the whole issue of time-varying and cross-sectional variation in risk premiums.

T-bonds, no reframing of the ERP Puzzle has occurred; there has been no questioning of why the recent risk premium is far *lower* than finance theory would suggest. Evidently, for many observers a history supported by soaring valuation multiples (and plunging dividend yields) is fair game for bolstering the forward-looking ERP, while a plunge in valuation multiples (and a huge jump in dividend yields) should be ignored in setting that same forward-looking ERP.

If the historical norm for the *expectational* ERP has been roughly half as large as the observed excess return from that rather special span of 1926–2000, the ERP Puzzle remains unsolved, but it is a bit less puzzling. If 100 people are polled on their appetite for equity market risk (I have done this informally many times), almost everyone will be found to eagerly embrace equity market risk if they truly believe that they will earn a 5 percent excess return over bonds, on a long-term compounded basis. That appetite diminishes with a shrinking ERP. The breakeven point, where half of the 100 people will choose *not* to hold an equity-centric portfolio, tends to center on roughly a 2 percent gap or a little more. That percentage point difference is the same ERP that Bernstein and I identified as the historical "normal" ERP in our 2002 article. Hardly anyone will want an equity-centric portfolio if they truly believe that they will garner only 1 percentage point more than long bonds or TIPS.

In our polling experiments, I venture to state that we would find almost no "votes" for accepting equity risk for the few 10ths of a percent incremental return for stocks that finance theory would justify. No one wants 15 percent annual volatility (compounding to about 50 percent total volatility over a 10-year span) if the expected annual return for all the risk is only about 0.5 percent more than the return for bonds.[4]

If market inefficiencies are firmly rooted in behavioral finance, it is easier to close a 2 percent gap than a 4 percent or 5 percent gap. The ERP Puzzle is considerably less puzzling.

Stocks for the Long Run? Yes, but How Long?

For most people, "slender" is an attractive goal.[5] For investors, however, a slender return or a slender risk premium is not at all attractive. For those seeking investments that are priced to offer material benefits to compensate for risk— a solid risk premium—bigger is better.

Few serious observers of the capital markets would argue that the future risk premium for stocks relative to bonds can rival the lofty excess return that stocks have delivered in the past. In the 85 years covered by the Ibbotson data, stocks delivered a real return of 6.6 percent, against 2.1 percent for bonds.

---

[4]By "total volatility," I mean 10-year (not annualized) lognormal volatility.
[5]This section is excerpted and amended from Arnott (2004).

Terrific! But a big part of this return is attributable to the past increase in the value that the market attaches to each dollar of earnings or dividends. Most observers would think subtracting expansion in the valuation multiple would be reasonable when framing future return expectations.

Using the growth of $100 over time, **Figure 2** breaks the total return on equities into its constituent parts.[6] Panel A does so for the 209 years from 1802 to 2010, and Panel B does so for the 85-year span covered by the Ibbotson data.

For the 209-year time span, the total return is 7.9 percent and the breakdown is as follows:

- *4.9 percent from dividends.* Suppose an investor received only the dividend yield, with no price appreciation, no growth in dividends, and no inflation contributing to price and dividend growth. Then, the investor's $100 would be worth $2.1 million in 2010. Pretty good.

- *1.5 percent from inflation.* Suppose an investor participated only in the part of the capital gain that came from inflation—no income, no growth in income, and no rising valuation multiples. This investor's $100 would have grown to $2,200 by 2010: The cost of living has risen 22-fold, according to U.S. Consumer Price Index statistics. Of course, the $2,200 would buy only what $100 would have bought in 1802 (by definition of "inflation").

- *0.8 percent from real growth in dividends.* Suppose an investor gave away his or her income, experienced no inflation, and did not participate in rising valuation levels but did participate in the real growth in the dividends from stocks. This investor would now have $552—after many more than 200 years. That amount is far less than most people would have expected.

- *0.5 percent from rising valuation multiples (hence, falling yields).* Suppose an investor received no income, saw no growth, and suffered no inflation but did have assets rise with the rise in equity valuation levels. This investor would have had $100 grow to $265 because dividend yields fell to 35 percent of their 1802 levels [or, viewed in terms of valuation multiples, price-to-dividend ratios (P/Ds) rose to nearly three times the 1802 levels]. P/Es saw a similar increase.

- *0.2 percent from compounding of the multiple sources of return.*

The total return from equities for 1926–2010 is 9.9 percent, and the breakdown is similar to that in Panel A:

- *4.1 percent from dividends.*

- *3.0 percent from inflation.*

---

[6]Figure 2 updates Arnott (2003).

Figure 2.   Attribution of Stock Market Returns
(lognormal scale)

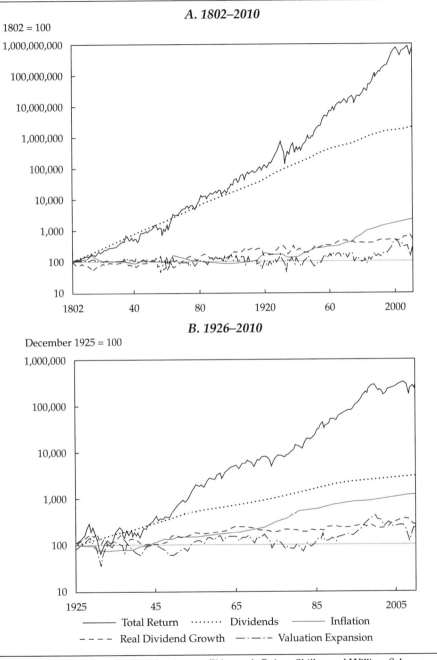

A. 1802–2010

B. 1926–2010

Total Return ········· Dividends ———— Inflation
– – – – Real Dividend Growth —·—·– Valuation Expansion

Source: Based on data from CRSP, Morningstar (Ibbotson), Robert Shiller, and William Schwert.

- *1.3 percent from real growth in dividends.*

- *1.1 percent from rising valuation levels.*

- *0.4 percent from compounding.*

For the full 209-year span starting in 1802, the 7.9 percent total return for stocks compares with 5.1 percent for long-term government bonds, giving us a 209-year excess return of 2.7 percent (net of compounding). Over the 85-year Ibbotson span, the long-term bond return is 5.2 percent and stock market excess return is 4.4 percent (again, net of compounding). If we take out the historical rise in valuation level—0.5 percent and 1.1 percent, respectively—these excess returns shrink to 2.2 percent for the longer period and 3.3 percent for the 85-year span.

Details of the impact of a "new normal" (in which GDP growth is impeded by the triple threat of deficits, debt, and demographics) on the ERP are beyond the scope of this paper. I would like to observe, however, that as people live longer and work longer, they have more time to accumulate wealth in anticipation of retirement. This phenomenon should lead investors to accept lower forward-looking stock and bond market returns and a lower risk premium for stocks. This phenomenon may be the cause of Japan's low current yield for both stocks and bonds and the steady erosion in these yields in the United States. It may also help explain investors' tolerance of low sovereign yields—even in the face of steadily escalating debt burdens and escalating fears of eventual defaults. Apparently, the risk premium should be lower than the historical 2–3 percent excess return, and a lower risk premium is wholly consonant with lower long-term return expectations for both stocks and bonds.

Let's explore the consequences of a slender risk premium. If stocks always offered a 5 percent risk premium relative to bonds, then no long-term investor would diversify away from stocks. The arithmetic is compelling. If stocks normally delivered better returns than bonds by 5 percent per year compounded over time, the long-term investor would have almost a 95 percent chance of winning with stocks by the end of a 20-year span. The cult of equities and the notion of stocks for the long run are predicated on such a lofty risk premium. If the risk premium is smaller, then the arithmetic quickly becomes drastically less interesting: If the risk premium falls by half, the time required to have high confidence of winning with stocks quadruples. The arithmetic is simple but powerful.[7]

Consider a disaster scenario for an investor—the 5th percentile outcome. **Figure 3** shows the 5th percentile relative wealth outcome for various risk premiums over time. In Panel A, if the difference in returns between stocks and

---

[7]I am indebted to André Perold for pointing out that if the risk premium falls by half, the time required to have high confidence of winning with stocks quadruples.

bonds is 5 percent and has a volatility of 15 percent, then the 5th percentile outcome is a 19 percent shortfall of stocks relative to bonds after one year.[8] That is, the investor would have a 5 percent chance of stocks underperforming bonds by 19 percent or more in a year. But over two years, the 5th percentile outcome is *not* another loss of 19 percent after the initial loss of 19 percent. Because risk expands with the square root of time, the 5th percentile outcome over two years is 34 percent below the mean. But the mean return has now grown another 5 percent, to a 10 percent gain. Thus, the 5th percentile outcome is a loss of only 24 percent over the two years, barely 5 percent worse than the one-year case.

In fact, if stocks can reasonably be expected to deliver 5 percent more than bonds, the "worst-reasonable" (or 5th percentile) outcome is that the equity investor is underwater relative to bonds by 26 percent after five years and never falls any lower. After five years, the picture becomes brighter. And, after 25 years, the investor has a better than 95 percent chance of winning with stocks, relative to bonds. In a nutshell, this kind of analysis is the basis for recommending stocks for the long run.

Unfortunately, some time periods, including the past decade, delivered far worse outcomes than a mere 26 percent peak-to-trough relative performance drawdown. If long-term bonds yield 4 percent, an investor needs to get a long-term return of 9 percent from stocks to get a 5 percent risk premium. If stocks are yielding 2 percent and if stocks have to return 9 percent, then stocks must deliver long-term earnings and dividend growth of 7 percent above the dividend yield. Such performance is a lot to ask. Annual per share earnings growth in the 20th century (no slacker for growth as centuries go) averaged slightly more than 4 percent, of which fully 3 percent was inflation.

Suppose earnings growth is only 4 percent, or 3 percent, or 2 percent. These growth rates, added to a 2 percent dividend yield, will correspond to a (respective) 6 percent, 5 percent, and 4 percent total return and, therefore, a (respective) 2 percent, 1 percent, and zero risk premium. After 25 years, the 5th percentile bleak outcome has the equity investor, respectively, 50 percent, 60 percent, and 70 percent behind the bond investor and still headed south. This bad news is the 5th percentile outcome, but it is well within the realm of possibility.

With smaller risk premiums, the shortfalls can be larger and it takes longer to recover. For example, Panel B shows that the worst-reasonable outcome for a 2 percent risk premium reaches about a 50 percent shortfall, and the equity investor finally has 95 percent confidence that stocks will beat bonds in 150

---

[8]The 5th percentile is 1.6 standard deviations below the mean. The standard deviation of 15 percent times 1.6 results in a 5 percent chance of having stocks perform 24 percent below this 5 percent mean outperformance, for a shortfall of 19 percent relative to bonds.

years. This point is also about the time that the worst-reasonable outcome with a 1 percent risk premium hits its low point, at 77 percent less wealth than the bond investor has. At this risk premium, the equity investor is still way behind bonds after 200 years in the 5 percent outcome.

In short, stocks work for the long run if the risk premium is large. But the "normal" risk premium over the past two centuries has been shown to be about 2.4 percent (Arnott and Bernstein 2002) and, if the same technology is used as in the 2002 paper, would be about 1.4 percent today. If the long-term average of 2.4 percent is right, then 100-year investors can expect their stocks to beat their bonds with 95 percent confidence. If the current risk premium is lower than 2.4 percent, the investor will need a longer horizon to have this much confidence in the superiority of the stock holdings.

Naturally, if the investor is willing to settle for a 60 percent likelihood of success, the span needed to wait for success is considerably shorter. But the myth is that a reasonable span for patient investors is all that is needed for stocks to assuredly outpace bonds. This myth is simply untrue unless stocks are priced to deliver a large risk premium relative to bonds.

The Myth of Buybacks

The bull market of the 1990s was built largely on a foundation of two immense misconceptions.[9] Investors were told the following:

1. With the coming of the technology revolution and a "new paradigm" of low payout ratios and internal reinvestment, earnings will grow faster than ever before. Real growth of 5 percent will be easy to achieve.[10]

2. When earnings are not distributed as dividends and not reinvested into stellar growth opportunities, they are distributed back to shareholders in the form of stock buybacks, which are a vastly preferable way of distributing company resources to the shareholders from a tax perspective.[11]

The vast majority of the institutional investing community has believed these untruths and has acted accordingly. Whether these myths are lies or merely errors, they are serious and demand scrutiny. Let's examine reinvestment first.

---

[9]This section is excerpted and amended from Bernstein and Arnott (2003).

[10]Like the myth of Santa Claus, this story is highly agreeable but is supported by neither observable current evidence nor history. Asness and I debunked this idea in a 2003 article (Arnott and Asness 2003). The work of Miller and Modigliani (1961) is often used as theoretical justification for this claim, although their capital equivalence theorem makes a typical array of simplifying assumptions (market efficiency, no taxes, free trading, etc.) not found in the real world. Furthermore, their work applies cross-sectionally.

[11]Bernstein and I demonstrated that stock repurchases rarely exceed new share issuance. The norm appears to be a "Two Percent Dilution" (Bernstein and Arnott 2003).

Figure 3. The Arithmetic of Long-Term Returns in the United States: 5th Percentile Relative Wealth Outcomes vs. Equity Risk Premiums

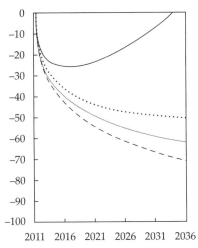

A. Twenty-Five Years

5th Percentile Outcome of Stocks vs. Bonds (%)

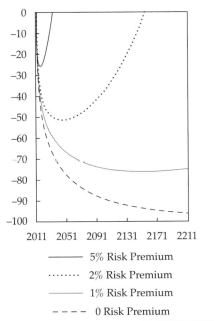

B. Two Hundred Years

5th Percentile Outcome of Stocks vs. Bonds (%)

———— 5% Risk Premium

········ 2% Risk Premium

———— 1% Risk Premium

– – – – 0 Risk Premium

I would not dispute the attractions of stock buybacks. They are a tax-advantaged way to provide a return on shareholder capital, particularly when compared with dividends, which are taxed twice. Buybacks have enormous appeal. Contrary to popular belief, however, apart from brief spans in the 1980s and the latest decade, they have not occurred to any meaningful degree in the past 85 years.

I suggest a simple measure of net new issuance—namely, the ratio of the proportionate increase in market capitalization to the proportionate increase in price. For example, if over a given period the market cap increased by a factor of 10 and the cap-weighted price index increased by a factor of 5, then 100 percent net share issuance has taken place in the interim.

This relationship has the advantage of factoring out valuation changes and splits because they are embedded in both the numerator and denominator. Furthermore, it holds only for universal market indices, such as the CRSP Cap-Based Portfolio indices 1–10, because less inclusive indices can vary the above ratio simply by adding or dropping securities. **Figure 4** shows the growth of $100.00 in total market cap and in the price of the CRSP 1–10. Note that even the CRSP data can involve adding securities: CRSP added the American Stock Exchange in 1962 and NASDAQ stocks in 1972.

Figure 4. Growth of U.S. Stock Prices and Capitalization, 1926–2010
(lognormal scale)

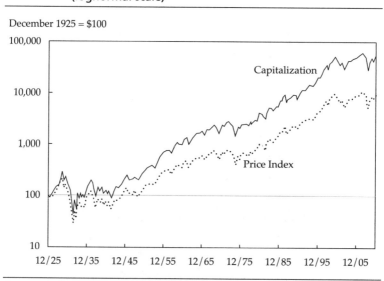

Source: Based on CRSP data.

An initial public offering (IPO) or a secondary equity offering (SEO) dilutes investors in the broad index. A buyback that reduces a company's outstanding float increases existing shareholders' ownership of the company. A buyback that merely offsets management stock option redemption—a common so-called buyback—is a wash; it does not change the float, so it is not a true buyback.

Note in Figure 4 how market cap slowly and gradually pulls away from market price. The gap does not look large in this figure, but by the end of 2010, the U.S. market cap index had grown 567-fold whereas the price index had grown only 101-fold. The reason for this discrepancy is simple: 82 percent of today's stock market consists of businesses that did not exist in 1925. For every share of stock extant in 1926, there are now 5.65 shares. These data imply net new share issuance at an annualized rate of slightly more than 2 percent per year.

To give a better idea of how this phenomenon has proceeded over the past 85 years, **Figure 5** shows a plot of a dilution index, defined as the ratio of capitalization growth to price index growth. (The adjustment for the stock additions of 1962 and 1972 is evident in Figure 5, where the dilution ratio was held constant for the two months during which the shifts took place.) Figure 5 traces the growth in the ratio of (1) the total capitalization of the CRSP 1–10 to (2) the market value–weighted price appreciation of these same stocks. The fact that this line rises nearly monotonically shows clearly that new share issuance almost always sharply exceeds stock buybacks. The notable exceptions are in the late 1980s, when buybacks outstripped new share issuance, and in the mid-2000s, when a flurry of demand from shareholders for buybacks occurred. That stock buybacks were an important force in the 1990s is simply a myth. The *belief* that stock buybacks were happening at an unprecedented pace may have been an important force, however, in the bull market of the 1990s.

Figure 6 shows the rolling 1-, 5-, and 10-year growth in the aggregate supply of equity capital; hence, dilution of an index affects investors' ownership of the market portfolio. Keep in mind that every 1 percent rise in equity capital is a 1 percent rise in market capitalization in which existing shareholders did not (and could not) participate. Except for the 1980s, the supply growth was essentially never negative even on a 1-year basis. How the myth of stock buybacks gained traction after the 1980s is clear; it was such a pervasive pattern in those years that even the 10-year average rate of dilution briefly dipped negative. But then, during the late 1990s, stock buybacks were outstripped by new-share issuance at a pace that was exceeded only in the IPO binge of 1926–1930. This surge in the supply of new stock is evident whether we are looking at net new-share issuance on a 1-, 5-, or 10-year basis. A recent, 2005–2007, spate of buybacks brought back the illusion that stock buybacks are a normal means by which management rewards shareholders in a tax-advantaged fashion.

Figure 5.   CRSP U.S. Market Capitalization/Price, 1926–2010

December 1925 = 1

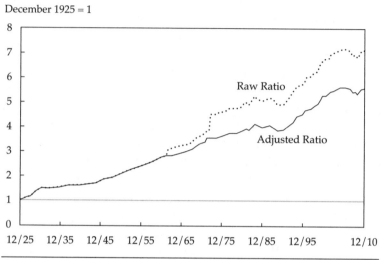

Source: Based on CRSP data.

Figure 6.   Annualized Rate of Shareholder Dilution in the United States, 1935–2010

Dilution (%)

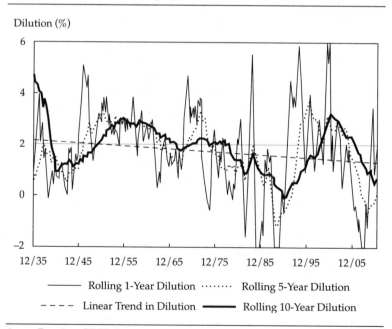

Source: Based on CRSP data.

Those who argue that stock buybacks will allow future earnings growth to exceed GDP growth can draw scant support from history. Could buybacks be large enough to be an important complement to dividends as a means of rewarding shareholders? Of course. Enormous earnings growth, far faster than real economic growth, did occur from 1990 to 2000. But much of this earnings growth was dissipated through shareholder dilution in the form of IPOs and SEOs.

Expected stock returns would be highly agreeable if dividend growth, and thus price growth, proceeded at the same rate as aggregate economic growth, or better. Unfortunately, this growth does not occur: Comparing the Dimson, Marsh, and Staunton (2002) 20th century dividend growth series with aggregate U.S. GDP growth, we find that even in nations that were not savaged by the century's tragedies, dividends grew, on average, 2.3 percent more slowly than the GDP. Similarly, by measuring the gap between the growth of market capitalization and share prices in the CRSP database, we find that between 1926 and the present, a 2.3 percent net annual dilution occurred in the outstanding number of shares in the United States.

Thus, two independent analytical methods point to the same conclusion: In stable nations, net annual creation of new shares is roughly 2 percent, which is the "2 percent dilution" that separates long-term economic growth from long-term per share dividend, earnings, and share price growth.

The Mythical Link of GDP Growth and Earnings Growth

Over the past two centuries, common stocks have provided a sizable excess return to U.S. investors: For the 200 years from 1802 through 2001, the returns for stocks, bonds, and bills were, respectively, 7.9 percent, 5.2 percent, and 4.2 percent. In the simplest terms, the reason is obvious: A bill or a bond is simply a promise to pay interest and principal, and as such, its upside is sharply limited. Shares of common stock, however, are a claim on the future dividend stream of the nation's businesses. The ever increasing fruits of innovation-driven economic growth accrue only to the shareholder, not the bondholder.

Viewed over the decades, this powerful economic engine produces remarkably even growth. **Figure 7** plots the real GDP of the United States since 1800. The economy, as measured by real GDP, has grown 1,300-fold since 1800, averaging about 3.5 percent per year. The long-term uniformity of economic growth is both a blessing and a curse. It is reassuring to know that real U.S. GDP has doubled every 20-odd years, partly on the basis of a rapidly growing population. But the data are also a dire warning to those predicting rapid acceleration of economic growth from the computer and internet revolutions. Such

Figure 7. Growth in U.S. Real GDP, Real per Capita GDP, Real Stock Price Return, Real Earnings, and Real Dividends
(lognormal scale)

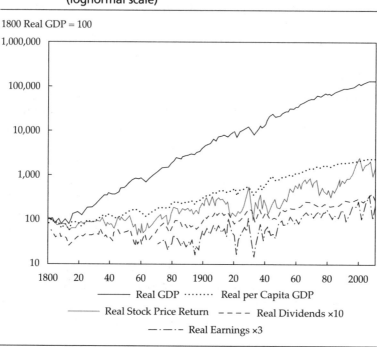

Source: Based on data from CRSP, Morningstar (Ibbotson), Robert Shiller, and William Schwert.

extrapolations of technology-driven increased growth are painfully oblivious to the broad sweep of scientific and financial history in which innovation and change are constant; they are neither new to the current generation nor unique. The technological advances of the 1990s register barely a blip on the long-term history shown in Figure 7; the travails of the past decade are far more noticeable.

The impact of recent advances in computer science pales in comparison with the technological explosion that occurred between 1820 and 1855. This earlier era contained the deepest and most far reaching technology-driven changes in everyday existence in human history. These changes profoundly affected the lives of those from the top to the bottom of society in ways that can scarcely be imagined today.

At a stroke, the speed of transportation increased tenfold and communications became almost instantaneous. Until 1820, people, goods, and information could not move faster than the speed of a horse. Within a generation, journeys achieved an order-of-magnitude less time, expense, danger, and discomfort because of steam, canals, and the railroad; important information that had previously required the same long journeys—taking weeks or months—could be transmitted instantaneously by telegraph.

Put another way, the average inhabitant of 1815 would have found the world of 40 years later incomprehensible, whereas a person transported from 1971 to 2011 would be duly impressed by our technological advances but would have little trouble understanding the intervening changes in everyday life (and would be shocked that we have not revisited the moon in 40 years!). From 1815 to 1855, the U.S. economy grew eightfold, whereas in the past 40 years, it has grown barely 150 percent.[12]

The relatively uniform increase in GDP is matched by a similar uniformity in the growth of corporate profits. A direct relationship has existed between aggregate corporate profits and GDP since 1871, the earliest market earnings data that anyone has assembled for U.S. stocks. Therefore, shouldn't stock prices have grown at the same rate? The problem is that per share earnings and dividends keep up with GDP only if no new shares are created. Unfortunately, entrepreneurial capitalism has a dilution effect; it creates new enterprises and new stock in existing enterprises so that *per share* earnings and dividends grow considerably more slowly than the economy, as Figure 7 shows.

In fact, as Figure 7 shows, since 1871, real stock prices have grown at 1.8 percent per year, versus 3.4 percent for real GDP. Furthermore, the true degree of "slippage" is much higher because one-third of the rise in real stock prices after 1871 was the result of a substantial upward revaluation (increase in the P/E or P/D). The highly illiquid industrial stocks of the post–Civil War period rarely sold at much more than 10 times earnings and often sold for multiples of only 3 to 4 times earnings. Those stocks gave way to the instantly and cheaply tradable common shares, priced many times more dearly, that we see today.

Note also in Figure 7 that real per share prices, earnings, and dividends grew at a pace similar to that of per capita GDP (with some slippage associated with the "entrepreneurial" stock rewards to management). Indeed, since 1871, these growth rates have been 1.8 percent for real per share prices, 1.4 percent for earnings, 1.1 percent for dividends, and 1.9 percent for GDP. Why should these rates be so tightly linked? Per capita GDP is a measure of productivity (with slight differences for changes in the workforce, hours worked, and so forth). And aggregate GDP per capita must grow in reasonably close alignment with productivity growth. Productivity growth is also the key driver for per capita income growth and for per share earnings and dividends. Accordingly,

---

[12]Of course, much of the growth in earlier GDP was driven by population growth, especially in the 1815–55 span. Still, per capita real GDP doubled in 1815–1855 but rose only by slightly more than 60 percent in the past 40 years.

any difference in the growth rates of GDP and the other three measures will mean that capital is deriving outsized benefits from productivity growth relative to labor (and vice versa). If share prices, earnings, and dividends grow faster than productivity, return on labor migrates to return on capital; if slower by a margin larger than the value of stock awards to management, then the economy is migrating from rewarding capital to rewarding labor. Either way, such a change in the orientation of the economy cannot continue indefinitely. The migration of returns to capital is corrected by a labor backlash; the migration of returns to labor by a flight of capital.

This observation has sobering implications at a time when corporate profits are near an all-time record high share of GDP and wages are near an all-time low share, as was the case in 2007 and again in 2011. Any student of market history will see that mean reversion is a powerful force in the interplay between these measures.

Is the United States unique? In their book *Triumph of the Optimists,* Dimson, Marsh, and Staunton (2002) tracked stock, bond, and cash returns over the previous century in 16 countries. I compared dividend growth, price growth, and total return with data on GDP growth and per capita GDP growth for the 16 countries covered by Dimson et al. (2002) in the 20th century. The GDP data come from Maddison's (2001) world GDP survey for 1900–1998 and the International Finance Corporation for 1998–2000. For the average country, there is a startling gap of 3.3 percent between dividend growth and the growth rate of aggregate GDP. For per capita GDP growth, there is still a 2.4 percent annual shortfall between dividend growth and per capita GDP growth. In the 2010 update of the Dimson et al. study, the results changed little.

The 20th century was not without turmoil. In our 2003 study, Bernstein and I divided 16 nations (see Bernstein and Arnott 2003) into two categories according to the degree of devastation visited upon them by the era's calamities. One group included countries that suffered substantial destruction of their productive physical capital at least once during the century; the other group did not. The nine nations in the first group were devastated in one or both of the world wars or by civil war. The remaining seven suffered relatively little direct damage.

For the nations that were devastated during the world wars or revolutions, the good news is that their economies repaired the devastations by the end of the 20th century. They enjoyed overall GDP growth and per capita GDP growth that rivaled the growth of the less scarred nations. The bad news is that the same cannot be said for per share equity performance. A slippage of 4.1 percentage points occurred between the annual growth rates of their economies and per share corporate payouts.

In the fortunate group—those untroubled by war, political instability, and government confiscation of wealth—we nevertheless found, on average, dividend growth 2.3 percentage points less than GDP growth and 1.1 percentage points less than per capita GDP growth. These results are similar to the 2.7 percent and 1.4 percent figures observed in the United States during the 20th century.

Why Does the Finance Industry Think Dividends Don't Matter?

Two misconceptions about the ERP that I stated in the opening are linked to the prevailing view that dividends aren't especially important. Respected academics have suggested the following:

1. If dividend yields are below historical norms, the market is clearly expecting faster future growth. (With this circular logic, we might as well buy at any valuation multiple because our buying creates still higher multiples and the resulting lower yields will imply even faster future growth.)

2. If payout ratios are below historical norms, the retained earnings will be reinvested in projects that will lead to faster future growth. (M&M are thus invoked. If that shortcut is sound, why not encourage management to retain all of the earnings? After all, the massive technological investments between 1998 and 2001, which were funded out of retained earnings, certainly must have led to a major step-up in subsequent earnings growth rates.)

A careful examination of the data provides no support for this intertemporal interpretation of M&M. Miller and Modigliani (1961) developed a brilliant thesis proving that dividend policy and structural debt/equity decisions do not matter so long as investors are rational, markets are efficient, there are no taxes, management operates in the best interests of the shareholders, bankruptcy costs are ignored, and so forth. These arguments seem to be tacitly based on the notion that because our "best" finance models (those that most accurately explain and predict phenomena) rely on certain assumptions, the assumptions must also be right. Even the best finance theories and models, however, rely on assumptions that are deliberate simplifications of the real world. Accordingly, even M&M's assumptions must be considered approximations of the real world.[13]

---

[13]Paul Samuelson said much the same: "Only the smallest fraction of economic writings, theoretical and applied, has been concerned with the derivation of *operationally meaningful* theorems. In part at least, this has been the result of the bad preconception that economic laws deduced from *a priori* assumptions possessed rigor and validity independently of any empirical human behavior. But only a very few economists have gone so far as this. The majority would have been glad to enunciate meaningful theorems if any had occurred to them." (Samuelson 1947, p. 3) [Italics in the original.]

When we approach the models, we can rely on common sense. Because the models are based on certain assumptions, we can examine the validity of those assumptions before we accept the dictates of the models as "truth."

Bond yields are accepted as the dominant factor in setting bond return expectations, but dividend yields (and, often, even earnings yields) are seen as secondary to growth in setting equity return expectations. Yet, overwhelming global evidence suggests a strong positive link between the dividend yield and both the subsequent real return for stocks and the subsequent excess return of stocks over bonds. It is a myth that in an efficient market investors will accept a lower yield whenever they are confident that future real growth in earnings will make up the difference. It is a myth that in an efficient market investors will not care about payout ratios because retained earnings make up for the deferred income in the form of more rapid growth; that is, lower dividends now mean higher ones later. These enduring myths lead to complacency about the ERP.

Conclusion: Why These Enduring Myths?

Why do we so readily accept forecasts based on extrapolating the past? If bond yields fall from 8 percent to 4 percent, and the bonds thereby deliver a 12 percent annualized return (including capital gains), should we assume 12 percent as a future bond return? Of course not! The capital gains that pushed the 8 percent yield up to a 12 percent return are nonrecurring. Should we "conservatively" assume a bit less than the historical 12 percent return—say, 10 percent—in recognition that yields are down? Of course not; the yield is 4 percent! So, the expected return is also 4 percent. Yet, much of our industry, with an assist from assorted academic luminaries, is wedded to forecasting equity returns by extrapolating past returns.

Returns are, for the most part, a function of simple arithmetic. For almost any investment, the total return consists of yield, growth, and multiple expansion or yield change. For bonds, the growth is simple: Fixed income implies zero growth. For high-yield or emerging market debt, growth is negative because of the occasional defaults. For stocks, based on a long history, growth tends to be around 1 percentage point above inflation.

The 7 percent real stock market returns of the past 78 years consist of roughly 4.3 percent from dividend yield, slightly more than 1 percent from real dividend growth, and 1.5 percent from multiple expansions. We cannot expect 7 percent in the future because we cannot rely on expansion of the multiple. Most observers would, at a minimum, subtract multiple expansions from future return expectations. Now, the return is down to about 5.5 percent. The current dividend yield, however, is only 1.6 percent, not 4.3 percent, which takes the real return down to around 2.5 percent to 3 percent. And that is without any "mean reversion" toward historical valuation levels. Much of our industry seems to prefer forecasting the future by extrapolating the past, however, because doing so produces a higher number.

Why is a low (even negative) risk premium considered shocking? Nothing assures a positive risk premium. Only finance theory (with numerous assumptions) suggests that this situation is not possible. But finance theory also posits that rational investors shun lotteries and casinos. Outside of finance theory, a temporary negative risk premium should be possible.

Should equity provide a positive risk premium relative to bonds? Of course. Is it written into contract law for any assets we buy? Of course not. In the long run, the market must adjust to provide a positive expected risk premium. But the adjustment to a positive rationally expected risk premium may be painful. A 5 percent risk premium is often taken as fact, but it is only a hypothesis and, many times, an ill-reasoned one.

Even the most aggressive, intellectually honest forecasts of long-term earnings or dividend growth assume GDP growth as an upper bound. Growth in the portion of GDP represented by corporate profits comes from the growth of existing enterprises and the creation of new enterprises. Stock market investments allow investors to participate in the former but not the latter. Because more than half of real GDP growth comes from entrepreneurial capitalism, real earnings and dividends should collectively grow a bit under half the rate of economic growth.

Nevertheless, consensus long-term earnings growth estimates routinely exceed sustainable GDP growth. The current consensus growth rate for earnings on the S&P 500, according to the Zacks Investment Research survey, is 10 percent, which, if we assume a consensus inflation expectation of 2–3 percent, corresponds to 7–8 percent real growth. Real earnings growth of 8 percent is six times the real earnings growth of the past century, however, and three times the consensus long-term GDP growth rate. This growth is not possible.

GDP growth, less the economic dilution associated with entrepreneurial capitalism, basically defines sustainable growth in per share earnings and dividends. Accordingly, it is hard to imagine that stocks offer a positive risk premium when they are yielding far less than TIPS. Yet, in December 1999 and January 2000, stock market yields were a scant 1.1 percent whereas the TIPS yield was 4.4 percent. Earnings and dividends on stocks would have needed to grow at 3.3 percent per year (triple the real growth rate of the prior century) for stocks to merely match the total return of TIPS. I believe a negative risk premium (at least for the broad stock market averages relative to TIPS) existed at the beginning of 2000.

Many market observers would agree that the cult of equities and reliance on a 5 percent ERP were the most damaging errors in the institutional sponsor community in the past quarter century. Shouldn't our industry, as a matter of course, question aggressive, unsustainable growth forecasts before acting on them?

Why do we accept rising return expectations in a rising market? In 1982, at a time when stock yields were 5 percent and both earnings yields and bond yields were in the low teens, the average pension return assumption was barely 6 percent. In 2000, the average pension return assumption had risen to approximately 9.5 percent, even though stock dividend yields and bond yields were down by, respectively, 4 percentage points and 8 percentage points. When markets fell in 2007–2009, we began to see pension return assumptions drifting downward again!

Siegel (2007) recognized that this mean reversion reduces the risk of equities for the long-term investor. A puzzle that he does not acknowledge is that, following the largest equity revaluation in history in 1982–2000, mean reversion might exact consequences in the form of reduction of future returns.

Too often, analysts rely on finance theory as a shortcut to easy answers. We point to M&M to reassure ourselves that 70 percent or even 100 percent earnings retention is fine because the retained earnings are surely being used to fund innovations that will lead to unprecedented future growth. We point to the capital asset pricing model (CAPM) to compute expected rates of return and to assess the alphas of our strategies. But none of these remarkable models and theories fully capture reality. Behavioral finance, the principal rival to the models of neoclassical finance theory, helps us understand how human frailties can create the very market behaviors that classical finance theory seeks to explain away, but behavioral finance does not help us decide how to profitably invest.

Our industry, in both the academic and the practitioner communities, is too complacent. Too many people say, "Assuming this, then we can decide that." Too few are willing to question their basic assumptions. As fiduciaries, we owe it to our clients to be less accepting of dogma and more willing to explore the implications of errors in the root assumptions of finance theory. These basic assumptions often fail when they are tested. Failing assumptions are not bad; indeed, that is where the profit opportunities can be found.

If finance theory assumes that markets are efficient and behavioral finance suggests that markets are not efficient, do we discard the less convenient theory? Isn't it better to recognize elements of truth in seemingly incompatible theories? Economics is not physics. Classical finance and behavioral finance *can* both be partially correct. If we recognize this possibility, we gain a rich understanding of the markets in which we seek our clients' profits and our livelihood.

REFERENCES

Arnott, Robert D. 2003. "Dividends and the Three Dwarfs." *Financial Analysts Journal*, vol. 59, no. 2 (March/April):4–6.

———. 2004. "The Meaning of a Slender Risk Premium." *Financial Analysts Journal*, vol. 60, no. 2 (March/April):6–8.

Arnott, Robert D., and Clifford S. Asness. 2003. "Surprise! Higher Dividends = Higher Earnings Growth." *Financial Analysts Journal*, vol. 59, no. 1 (January/February):70–87.

Arnott, Robert D., and Peter L. Bernstein. 2002. "What Risk Premium Is 'Normal'?" *Financial Analysts Journal*, vol. 58, no. 2 (March/April):64–85.

Bernstein, Peter. 1997. "What Rate of Return Can You Reasonably Expect... or What Can the Long Run Tell Us about the Short Run?" *Financial Analysts Journal*, vol. 53, no. 2 (March/April):20–28.

Bernstein, William J., and Robert D. Arnott. 2003. "Earnings Growth: The Two Percent Dilution." *Financial Analysts Journal*, vol. 59, no. 5 (September/October):47–55.

Campbell, John Y., and John H. Cochrane. 1999. "By Force of Habit: A Consumption-Based Explanation of Aggregate Stock Market Behavior." *Journal of Political Economy*, vol. 107, no. 2 (April):205–251.

Campbell, John Y., and Robert J. Shiller. 1988. "The Dividend-Price Ratio and Expectations of Future Dividends and Discount Factors." *Review of Financial Studies*, vol. 1, no. 3 (Autumn):195–228.

Cochrane, John H. 2011. "Presidential Address: Discount Rates." *Journal of Finance*, vol. 66, no. 4 (August):1047–1108.

Dimson, Elroy, Paul Marsh, and Mike Staunton. 2002. *Triumph of the Optimists: 101 Years of Global Investment Returns*. Princeton, NJ: Princeton University Press.

———. 2010. *Global Investment Returns Yearbook 2010*. Zurich: Credit Suisse Research Institute.

Fama, Eugene F., and Kenneth R. French. 1988. "Dividend Yields and Expected Stock Returns." *Journal of Financial Economics*, vol. 22, no. 1 (October):3–25.

———. 1992. "The Cross-Section of Expected Stock Returns." *Journal of Finance*, vol. 47, no. 2 (June):427–465.

———. 1993. "Common Risk Factors in the Returns on Stocks and Bonds." *Journal of Financial Economics*, vol. 33, no. 1 (February):3–56.

Hirshleifer, Jack, Amihai Glazer, and David Hirshleifer. 2005. *Price Theory and Applications: Decisions, Markets, and Information*. Cambridge, U.K.: Cambridge University Press.

Ibbotson, Roger G., and Rex A. Sinquefield. 1977. *Stocks, Bonds, Bills, and Inflation: The Past (1926–1976) and the Future (1977–2000)*. Charlottesville, VA: The Financial Analysts Research Foundation.

Maddison, Angus. 2001. *The World Economy: A Millennial Perspective*. Washington, DC: Organisation for Economic Co-Operation and Development.

Miller, Merton, and Franco Modigliani. 1961. "Dividend Policy, Growth, and the Valuation of Shares." *Journal of Business*, vol. 34, no. 4 (October):411–433.

Samuelson, P. 1947. *Foundations of Economic Analysis*. Cambridge, MA: Harvard University Press.

Siegel, Jeremy J. 2006. "The 'Noisy Market' Hypothesis." *Wall Street Journal* (14 June):A14.

———. 2007. *Stocks for the Long Run: The Definitive Guide to Financial Market Returns & Long Term Investment Strategies*. 4th ed. New York: McGraw-Hill.

Taleb, Nassim. 2007. *The Black Swan: The Impact of the Highly Improbable*. 1st ed. New York: Random House.

Time Variation in the Equity Risk Premium

Antti Ilmanen

Managing Director
AQR Capital Management (Europe) LLP

The equity risk premium (ERP) refers to the (expected; sometimes, realized) return of a broad equity index in excess of some fixed-income alternative. In the past decade, a dramatic shift has occurred in what is considered to be the best source of information about the future ERP: Is it historical average returns or forward-looking valuation indicators?

- Academics and practitioners alike used to think that the ERP is constant over time, in which case the future premium would best be estimated from the long-run average of the realized excess return. If the historical realized outperformance of stocks over bonds was 6 percent, for example, 6 percent would also be the best forecast for the future. Such a rearview-mirror perspective makes the ERP seem especially high at the end of each long bull market, just when market valuation ratios are abnormally high.

- The recent roller-coaster experiences in markets, as well as theoretical and empirical lessons, have converted many observers to the belief that expected returns and premiums vary over time. If so, then past average returns are a highly misleading indicator of future returns. Forward-looking valuation indicators are better and may provide useful timing signals. Low dividend yields or low earnings yields (or their inverse, high price-to-earnings ratios) are now seen as a sign of low prospective stock market returns in just the same way that low bond yields and narrow yield spreads are interpreted as a forecast of low returns in fixed-income markets. This forward-looking logic would have guided investors well during the low equity market yields of 2000 and high market yields of early 2009.

This shift in opinion can also be described as a change in the perceived information in market yields (valuation ratios). Does a low dividend yield in the equity market predict low future returns (reflecting low required risk premiums or investor irrationality) or high future cash flow growth (reflecting growth optimism)? The answer must be one or the other—or some combination of the two. Empirical research has shown that low dividend yields tend to precede subpar market returns rather than above-average growth. In January 2011 in Denver, John Cochrane of the University of Chicago, in the American

Finance Association's presidential address (see Cochrane 2011), argued that a 100 percent reversal had occurred in academic thinking on this question in the past 20–30 years. Cochrane explained the following:

- The ERP is no longer thought to be constant *over time*. All time variation in market valuation ratios was once thought to reflect changing growth expectations (with an unchanging *ex ante* required risk premium), but now all such variation is thought to reflect changing required returns.

- All expected return variation *across stocks* was thought to reflect stocks' differing betas. Now, the beta is thought to explain none of the cross-sectional variation in expected returns.

Not all academics agree. Some harbor doubts about return predictability and argue that the evidence against a constant risk premium is limited. For example, variation in the ERP could be sample specific or reflect subtle econometric problems in predictability regressions.[1] And those who agree that expected returns vary over time have a follow-up debate over whether this time variation reflects rational drivers (such as wealth-dependent risk aversion), varying amounts of risk in the market, or investor irrationality.

Practitioner thinking has experienced similar shifts. Many investors have become open to the idea of market timing since the decade of boom-to-bust cycles, when forward-looking valuation indicators turned out to give decent forecasts. Yet, even if a time-varying ERP reflects a general tendency for investor risk aversion to rise in bad times, the typical investor should not necessarily become a contrarian market timer. As many investors found out in 2008, their risk appetites fell at least as fast as their wealth, so they did not feel inclined to jump at the bargains (low market valuations, high expected returns). Investors with a longer horizon or relatively stable risk preferences may well be the more natural buyers when such contrarian opportunities arise. Even for them, however, exploiting high expected returns is not easy because no one knows when the market will hit bottom—until after the fact.

Before we turn to forward-looking market analysis, consider the historical equity market performance over the past 111 years shown in **Table 1**. The geometric average excess return of stocks over long-term government bonds has been more than 4 percent in the United States but a bit lower in the rest of the world. (The excess returns would be higher if stocks were compared with short-dated U.S. T-bills or if arithmetic averages were used.) Equities have outperformed bonds in all of the markets Dimson, Marsh, and Staunton (2011) studied. The 20th century may have been especially favorable, however, for stocks versus bonds; the return gap for the 19th century was less than 1 percent in the United States.

---

[1]Typical is the debate between Welch and Goyal (2008) and Campbell and Thompson (2008).

Table 1. Compound Annual (Geometric) Equity Returns and ERPs, 1900–2010

Market	Real Equity Return	ERP over Long-Term U.S. Government Bonds
United States	6.3%	4.4%
World ex-U.S. (in $)	5.0	3.8
World (in $)	5.5	3.8
Range among 19 markets	2.0–7.4%	2.0–5.9%

Source: Dimson, Marsh, and Staunton (2011).

My favorite valuation ratio for the equity market is the inverse of the "Shiller P/E10," which Yale Professor Robert Shiller conveniently updates each month on his website.[2] Because one-year earnings may be too volatile and cyclical for accurate comparisons, Shiller compares today's market prices with smoothed (10-year averages of real) earnings. **Figure 1** compares this ratio, which I'll henceforth call the "real E10/P" or just "E10/P," with the real long-term Treasury yield from January 1900 to February 2011.[3] The solid line correctly predicted high prospective returns for equities in the early 1920s, the 1930s, the 1980s, and more recently in late 2008–2009. Similarly, it captured the low prospective returns in 1929 and 2000, both in stand-alone equity investments and relative to bonds.

Framework to Anchor the Debates

The gap between the two lines in Figure 1 is roughly the forward-looking ERP. Yet, strictly speaking, the Shiller earnings yield equals the *ex ante* real return for equities only under fairly stringent conditions. The dividend discount model (DDM) provides a cleaner conceptual framework than the Shiller earnings yield for assessing the difference between the long-term expected returns of stocks and bonds. Analysts will, of course, debate the inputs of the model and the resulting ERP estimates, but this framework at least gives the debaters a common language.

In the basic version of the DDM, cash flows to equity investors (which can be considered, narrowly, to be dividends) are assumed to grow at a constant annual rate G. A feasible long-run return on equities is then the sum of the cash flow yield (here, dividend yield, or D/P) and the trend of cash flow growth rate,

[2]The P/E10 is the price or index value of the S&P 500 Index divided by the average of the last 10 years of earnings. Shiller's website is www.econ.yale.edu/~shiller/data.htm.

[3]In the real long-term Treasury yield, the nominal Treasury yield is deflated by the consensus forecast inflation for the next decade (for the period before survey forecasts became available in the 1970s, statistical estimates were used). For details, see Ilmanen (2011).

Figure 1. Smoothed Real Earnings Yields of U.S. Equities and *Ex Ante* Real Yields on 10-Year Treasuries, 1900–2011

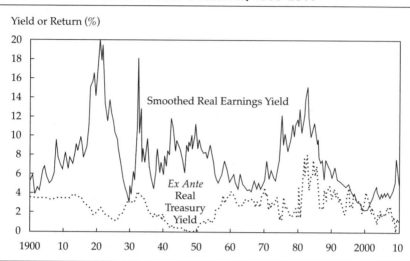

Sources: Bloomberg; Shiller website (www.econ.yale.edu/~shiller/data.htm); U.S. Federal Reserve; *Blue Chip Economic Indicators*, *Consensus Economics.*

G. The required return on equities, or the discount rate, can be viewed as the sum of the riskless long-term Treasury yield, *Y*, and the required equity-over-bond risk premium, the ERP. Intuitively, markets are in equilibrium when the equity market return that investors require, *Y* + *ERP*, equals the return that markets are able to provide, *D/P* + *G*. These expressions can be reshuffled to state the *ex ante* ERP in terms of three building blocks:

$$ERP = D/P + G - Y.$$

The DDM can be expressed in nominal terms (with G_{nom} and Y_{nom}) or in real terms (with G_{real} and Y_{real}) if both expected cash flow growth and the bond yield for expected inflation are adjusted. The model can also be expressed as an earnings discount model if a constant dividend payout rate is assumed. With a constant payout rate, the growth rates of dividends and earnings are equal.

The DDM framework can be easily extended to include a variety of short-term and long-term growth rates, but the use of the DDM to analyze time-varying ERPs can only be informal because it is a steady-state model that assumes constant expected returns and valuation ratios. In a dynamic variant of the DDM, one that allows time-varying expected returns, *D/P* is a combination of the market's expectations of future (required) stock returns and dividend growth (see Campbell and Shiller 1988).

©2011 The Research Foundation of CFA Institute

The DDM framework is simple and flexible, but what inputs to use in calculating the ERP is a topic of wide disagreement. Even the observable inputs—dividend yield and bond yield—are ambiguous because broader payout yields (including, for example, share buybacks) may be appropriate for equities and the maturity and nature (nominal versus real) of the Treasury yield may be debated. The main source of contention, however, is the assumed trend of the growth rate of profits, or earnings per share (EPS), *G*.

Nevertheless, this framework can be used to analyze the building blocks of realized and prospective equity market returns (see Ibbotson and Chen 2003). **Figure 2** decomposes the realized 110-year (1900–2009) compound annual U.S. stock market return of 9.6 percent into its elemental parts with separate decompositions for the "demand" and "supply" of returns. The nomenclature follows Diermeier, Ibbotson, and Siegel (1984). The total return is split into either

- the sum of returns demanded by the investor (the first column in Figure 2), on the assumption that sample averages capture required returns well: 4.7 percent nominal T-bond return + 4.7 percent *ex post* ERP + small interaction terms, represented by the black bands or

Figure 2. Decomposed Historical Equity Market Returns, 1900–2009

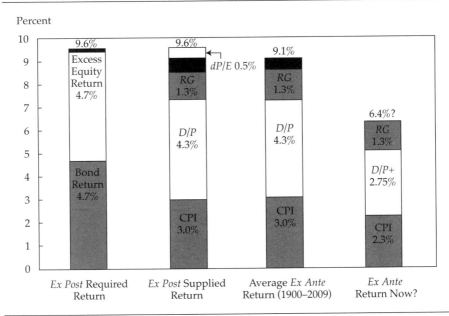

Note: RG = real earnings growth, *dP/E* = repricing gains, and CPI is the U.S. Consumer Price Index.
Sources: Arnott and Bernstein (2002); Bloomberg; Shiller website (www.econ.yale.edu/~shiller/data.htm).

- the sum of returns supplied by the economy (the second column in Figure 2): 3.0 percent average inflation + 4.3 percent average dividend yield + 1.3 percent average real EPS growth rate + 0.5 percent repricing effect (which represents the annualized impact of the expansion of the P/E by 75 percent—from 12.5 to 21.9—during the sample period) + small interaction terms.

The third column shows the result when, following Ibbotson and Chen, I deemed the 0.5 percent repricing gain to be an unexpected windfall and subtracted it from the supplied returns.[4] This column suggests, then, that investors required an *ex ante* nominal equity market return of 9.1 percent between 1900 and 2009, on average. If expected returns vary over time and current values differ from the average levels over the sample, this analysis can be misleading for assessing current expected returns. The current inflation rate and equity and bond yields are clearly below historical averages. Using a 2.3 percent rate of CPI growth (the consensus forecast for long-term inflation) and a 2.0 percent D/P produces a forward-looking measure predicting only 5.6 percent nominal equity returns. Admittedly, the D/P value could be higher if a broader carry measure that included net share buybacks were used, so for the last column in Figure 2, I added 0.75 percent to the estimate (and called it "$D/P+$"). Return forecasts more bullish than the 6.4 percent nominal return in the fourth column would have to rely on growth optimism (beyond the historical 1.3 percent rate of real EPS growth, to be discussed later) or further P/E expansion in the future (my analysis assumes none). More bearish forecasts consider my buyback adjustment excessive and/or my growth or valuation forecasts overly optimistic.

Figure 2 is based on data at the end of 2009. Conveniently, market changes over the subsequent 15 months have been modest. Equity markets have rallied somewhat, with dividend yields dropping from 2 percent to 1.8 percent (and the Shiller E10/P falling from 5 percent to 4.3 percent), whereas Treasury yields and consensus inflation forecasts are virtually unchanged.

So, when asked what I expect the realized outperformance of U.S. equities over Treasuries to be for the decade from the first quarter (Q1) of 2011 to Q1:2021, I pretty much stay with the same numbers. In **Exhibit 1**, I predict 4 percent real (compound annual) return for the equity market and 1 percent real return for Treasuries—close to the current 10-year yield of Treasury Inflation-Protected Securities (TIPS)—thus, a 3 percent ERP. Because inflation terms wash out across stocks and bonds, I do not need to forecast inflation, which is currently an especially hard call. I would assign a ±0.25 percent band around each component estimate.

---

[4]To be a stickler, I'll note that the yield and growth estimates are consistent only if the payout ratio is constant over time. I could use the real dividend growth rate (averaging 1.2 percent) and the repricing effect based on dividend yield changes (which has a slightly higher annualized impact, 0.7 percent) instead of earnings data, and I would obtain, broadly, the same results.

Exhibit 1. Components of the ERP

Component	Estimate for Next Decade
Equity cash flow yield	2.7% (*D/P* + addition for net buybacks)
+ Real cash flow growth	1.3 (historical average EPS growth)
+ Valuation change	0 (assume unchanged valuations)
− Real Treasury yield	−1
ERP	3%

For the global markets, my ERP forecast is similar. In most countries, I can see somewhat better growth prospects than in the United States, but these prospects are offset by higher real yields. Japan is the one exception; growth prospects are worse there than in the United States.

Debates about the Values of the Main Components

As I have stressed, these building blocks give us a useful framework for debating the values of key components of future ERPs. What are these debates?

Equity Market Yield. Dividend yield is the classic proxy for equity market yield. Having ranged between 3 percent and 6 percent for 40 years, the *D/P* of the S&P 500 Index fell below 3 percent in 1993 for the first time ever and then fell below 2 percent in 1997, remaining there for the next decade. The decline in the *D/P* in the 1980s and 1990s partly reflects a structural change: Many companies replaced dividends with repurchases (i.e., stock buybacks), which were more tax efficient and more flexible and which had a more positive impact on share price (and thereby executive compensation) than did dividends. One reason share buybacks increased is the 1982 change in U.S. SEC rules that provide a safe harbor from price manipulation charges for companies conducting share buybacks.

The obvious improvement in the measurement of the equity market yield would be to include share buybacks. The buyback yield never exceeded 1 percent before 1985 but did in most years thereafter. Even though the buyback yield has in some years exceeded the dividend yield, the buyback yield arguably should not get as high a weight as the dividend yield in any long-run yield measure because it is not as persistent. It is much easier for a corporation to reduce repurchase activities than to cut dividends.

Only adding share buybacks (i.e., not subtracting share issuance), as is sometimes done, would overstate the effective yield. Companies may repurchase shares or pay dividends when they have excess cash, whereas they issue "seasoned" equity when they need more capital from investors.

Cash-financed merger and acquisition deals are another component of cash flows to the investor that could be included in a broad yield measure. The literature on this issue is diverse, however, and hardly conclusive. In computing the net buyback-adjusted yield, net payout yield, and change in Treasury stock, somewhat different data are used to adjust dividend yields, but the intent of all of them is the same: to estimate total cash flow from the company to the investor (see Allen and Michaely 2003; Boudoukh, Michaely, Richardson, and Roberts 2007; Fama and French 2001).

Figure 3 plots one estimate of broader cash flow yield, the dividend yield, and the buyback yield over a quarter century. This broad yield estimate has not been systematically higher than the dividend yield; buybacks and issuance have roughly canceled out over time. Other estimates imply higher cash flow yields, especially since the mid-1990s, so I stay with the 0.75 percent addition over *D/P*. Some may deem this adjustment too high; others, too low. More empirical research is clearly needed.

Equity Cash Flow Growth. Some studies use growth estimates based on analyst expectations for earnings growth or on P/Es, for which they use analyst forecasts of next-year operating earnings. Both approaches embed analyst overoptimism and result in upwardly biased estimates of the ERP.

Figure 3. Equity Market Yield Measures, 1984–2009

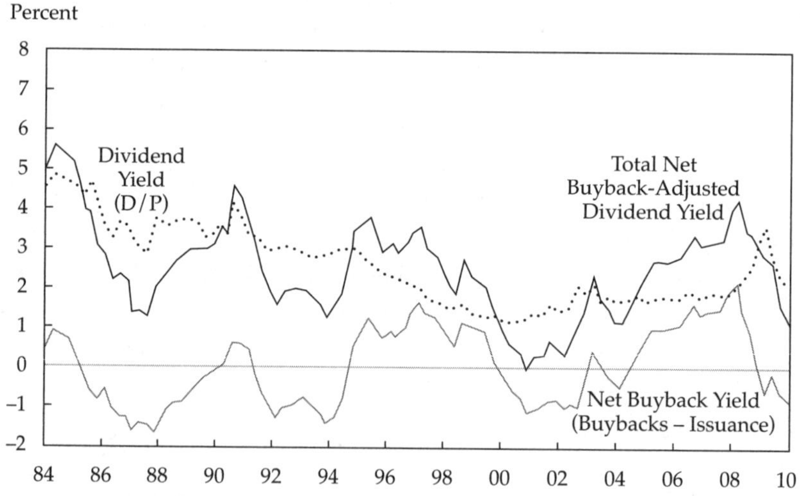

Sources: Haver Analytics; Nomura.

A more conservative approach is to use the trend of the rate of growth in real GDP or corporate profits.[5] Even this approach turns out to be overoptimistic. Although many practitioners think that the GDP growth rate is a *floor* for earnings and dividend growth, the rate has historically been a *ceiling* that has been broken only during benign decades. Arnott and Bernstein (2002), Bernstein and Arnott (2003), and Cornell (2010) showed that growth rates of per share earnings and dividends have, over long histories, lagged the pace of GDP growth and sometimes even per capita GDP growth. As **Table 2** shows, between 1950 and 2009, growth rates of earnings and dividends per share almost matched the 1.9 percent real growth rate of GDP per capita but clearly lagged real GDP growth (3.1 percent).

Table 2. Average Real Long-Term Growth Rates (Geometric Means), 1900–2009

Period	Real GDP	Real GDP per Capita	Real EPS	Real Dividends per Share
1900–1949	3.2%	1.8%	1.0%	1.0%
1950–2009	3.1	1.9	1.5	1.3

Sources: Arnott and Bernstein (2002); Haver Analytics.

Taking even longer histories does not help. The first half of the 20th century looked even worse for earnings and dividend growth. When I looked at shorter histories, I saw a prettier picture for a while. Between 1988 and 2007, U.S. real EPS growth averaged 3.7 percent a year—clearly larger than the real GDP growth rate (2.4 percent). This period was an exceptionally benign one, however, for capital markets; for example, the share of GDP represented by corporate profits rose from 8 percent to 11 percent. After 2008, the trailing 20-year real EPS growth rate was negative; after the 2009 recovery, it was still only 1.3 percent.

Studying the global evidence also does not help to raise the growth estimate. Dimson, Marsh, and Staunton (2002) showed that between 1900 and 2000, growth in real dividends per share lagged growth in real GDP per capita in 15 of the 16 countries they examined. Across countries, real dividend growth averaged nearly zero and lagged growth in real GDP per capita by 2.4 percentage points. U.S. dividend growth was somewhat better but still lagged growth in real GDP per capita by 1.4 percentage points.

---

[5]Some analysts use the trend in the growth of nominal earnings (say, 7 percent). By doing so, they conveniently forget that such nominal growth occurred over a period when inflation averaged 4 percent, whereas the current expected inflation is closer to 2 percent.

MSCI Barra (2010) has contrasted (real) EPS growth and GDP growth between 1969 and 2009 in 16 countries. The researchers found that, averaged across all the countries, annual GDP growth was 2.4 percent—compared with 0.1 percent EPS growth. (Comparable figures in the United States are 2.8 percent and 1.3 percent.) The gap in growth rates between GDP and EPS was positive (0.5–5.0 percent) in all the countries studied except Sweden.

Why? These patterns seem puzzling. In the long run, GDP and profits should have similar trends in growth rates; otherwise, the corporate sector would eventually dominate the economy. (Admittedly, this argument is only relevant over extremely long periods.) An important distinction must be made, however, between aggregate earnings growth and EPS growth. Aggregate earnings growth has matched GDP growth quite closely during the post–World War II era; EPS growth has not.

Investors in existing listed stocks capture only part of aggregate profit growth because a portion of this growth is financed with newly issued equity. Arnott and Bernstein (2002) stressed that new entrepreneurs and labor (including top management) capture a large share of economic growth at the expense of shareholders in existing companies. Stock market indices (made up of listed stocks) miss the most dynamic growth in the economy, which comes from unlisted start-up ventures, other small businesses, and sole proprietorships—all of which count toward total business profits.

Total corporate profit growth is, therefore, effectively diluted by net equity issuance. Cornell (2010) showed that the annual dilution rate (mainly through new business creation but also through net issuance by existing companies) between 1926 and 2008 was 2 percent and reasonably stable over time. Subtracting the 2 percent dilution effect from 3 percent real aggregate earnings growth makes 1 percent real EPS growth a realistic long-run prospect. Some evidence indicates, however, that the dilution effect has flattened during the past decade, perhaps reflecting the increasing use of buybacks.

Although several studies confirm these patterns, the crucial distinction between aggregate earnings growth and EPS earnings growth is not widely appreciated, and many ERP estimates rely on at least a 3 percent real trend in EPS growth. As Upton Sinclair said, "It is difficult to get a man to understand something, when his salary depends upon his not understanding it." Still, it is true that over a single decade, real EPS growth may deviate significantly from its long-run trend, so this building block can be subject to very vigorous debates.

Valuation Change. I have assumed here unchanged market valuations over the coming decade. It is often a good base assumption in normal circumstances.

One can argue, however, that current equity markets are expensive in an absolute sense. The Shiller P/E10 is near 23, more than 40 percent above its long-run average. The smoothed real earnings yield is only 4.3 percent (100/23), not far from the average of the bottom quintile over a 110-year history. **Figure 4** shows that real stock market returns have typically been modest in years following low starting yields (and high following high starting yields). Generally, Figure 4 indicates that this valuation ratio has the useful ability to predict future market returns.[6]

Other market valuation indicators suggest that equity markets are fairly valued. And in comparison with even more expensive Treasuries, the equity market may appear to be cheap.

Figure 4. Average Level of E10/P and Subsequent Returns by Periods, 1900–2009

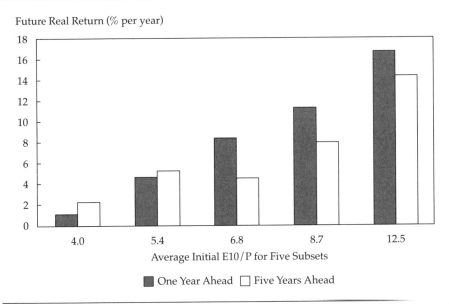

Notes: The graph was created by sorting each month into one of five buckets based on the level of real E10/P at the beginning of the month and then computing the average level for E10/P (*x*-axis labels) and subsequent one-year and five-year real stock market returns (*y*-axis values) in five subsets of the sample history. Real return is the S&P 500 return.

Sources: Shiller website (www.econ.yale.edu/~shiller/data.htm); Haver Analytics.

---

[6]The predictive ability is somewhat overstated because the sorting of months into quintiles uses in-sample information. Investors know only with hindsight that 4 percent earnings yields would be among the lowest and 12 percent yields among the highest during the full sample. The mean-reversion effect is, therefore, overstated.

In addition to market valuations, many other determinants of the outlook for growth and valuation can be considered. Bearish observers focus on debt problems, deleveraging, and unfavorable demographics. Bullish observers note that technological progress has tended to surprise on the upside and that widening knowledge and access to information may benefit from increasing returns to scale, unlike traditional capital, which tends to exhibit decreasing returns to scale.

I highlight one bearish consideration. High inflation tends to hurt equity markets, but so does deflation. Steady and low, but positive, inflation appears to be the optimal environment for real growth and risky-asset valuations. **Figure 5** shows a sombrero-shaped relationship between equity market valuation levels (P/E10) and inflation levels over the past 110 years. The sweet spot of peak valuations occurs with inflation in the 1–4 percent range. One mechanism behind this nonlinear relationship is that economic uncertainty—here measured by inflation volatility and equity market volatility—tends to be higher amid deflation and high inflation. Thus, inflation may not directly influence

Figure 5. U.S. Equity Market Valuations and Inflation, 1900–2009

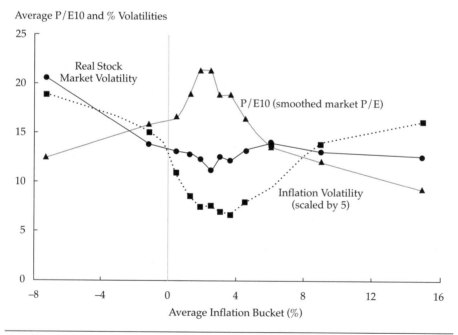

Note: The graph was created by sorting each month into 1 of 12 subsets on the basis of the level of inflation during the month and then computing the average level for inflation (*x*-axis), the P/E10 valuation ratio, and the two volatility series (*y*-axis) in the 12 subsets of the sample history.

Sources: Haver Analytics; Shiller website (www.econ.yale.edu/~shiller/data.htm); author's calculations.

equity market valuations, but it affects the market through its impact on economic growth and uncertainty. Whatever the reason, the pattern is bad news for market valuations because two decades have been at the sweet spot, so the likelihood of both deflation and high inflation for the coming decade has substantially increased.

Treasury Yield. This component is subtracted. Bonds appear at least as expensive as stocks when measured by historical yardsticks, especially in comparison with the past 30 or 60 years of experience. Moreover, the debt and demographic problems make many expert observers worry about inflation reaching levels not seen since the 1980s.

A perhaps surprising phenomenon is that current bond yields do not contain much of a risk premium. **Figure 6** clarifies this statement by decomposing the 10-year Treasury yield into three components: expected average inflation, expected average real T-bill rates, and the required bond risk premium over bills. The decomposition is based on consensus forecasts of next-decade average inflation and average T-bill rates. The current 10-year yield of 3.4

Figure 6. Decomposition of the 10-Year Treasury Yield Based on Survey Data, 1983–2011

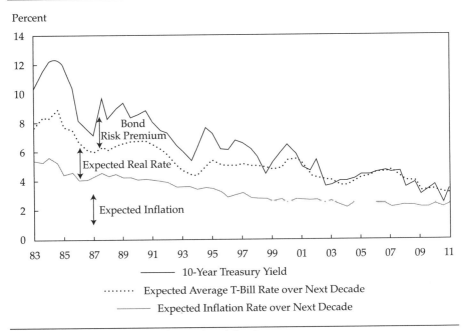

Note: Each year measurement is as of March and October.
Sources: Bloomberg; *Blue Chip Economic Indicators.*

percent is close to the average expected T-bill rate, implying a bond risk premium of nearly zero. Simply put, the yield curve is exceptionally steep, but all this steepness seems to reflect the market's expectation of short rates rising sharply from the abnormal near-zero level. The expected real yield on the nominal 10-year bond is slightly more than 1 percent, well below the past 30-year average of 3 percent. The 10-year TIPS has a yield slightly under 1 percent, but this yield is an average reflecting negative real yields at the front end and clearly higher real yields further out.

The reasons for Treasuries' continued richness include still-modest inflation; the exceptional safe-haven role of Treasuries in recessions, deflations, and financial crises (which has been extremely valuable in the past decade but may not work as well in the next decade); and various exceptional sources of demand (large asset purchases by the Fed, reserve accumulation by other central banks, and purchases by pension funds seeking close asset/liability matching).

I simply assume a 1 percent real bond return for the next decade, which is broadly in line with the current market pricing of both nominal and inflation-linked Treasuries. These yields are known today.

An alternative way of computing the ERP involves comparing stock returns with the returns of constant-maturity bonds (or of long-term bond indices) over time. If such a method is used, the results thus depend on future yield changes. Unexpectedly bond-bearish outcomes would probably also hurt equity market valuations. They might leave the realized excess return of stocks and bonds broadly unchanged, but with both asset classes earning real returns lower than the now expected, respectively, 4 percent and 1 percent.

Concluding Thoughts

In this paper, I focus on the prospects of the equity risk premium over the next decade. However, it is worthwhile to think about the *term structure* of such premiums. A world of time-varying expected returns contains more than one premium number. The short-run and long-run premiums can differ significantly. How would the forecast beyond 2021 differ from the prediction for the next decade?

- The term structure effects are more obvious on the bond side of the premium. Short-dated TIPS yields are currently negative (consistent with short-dated nominal Treasuries yielding nearly zero while headline inflation is nearly 2 percent and rising). At the same time, the 10-year TIPS yield is 0.9 percent and the 20–30 year TIPS yields are approaching 2 percent. Together, these yields imply a 2.7 percent forward TIPS yield for the decade starting in 2021.

- Abnormally high (or low) starting valuations for equity markets and related mean-reversion potential have strong implications for expected stock market returns for the next few years. When considering prospective equity returns *after* the next decade, however, it is impossible to know what the starting valuation levels will be in 2021. Thus, if one assumes below-average equity market returns for the next decade because of an expected normalization of the currently high Shiller P/E10, the best forecast for real equity market returns beyond 2021 should be close to the "unconditional" long-term return forecasts. That is, these "forward forecasts" should largely ignore starting valuations (or at least allow future higher starting yields in 2021 than in 2011).

- Many indicators in addition to valuation measures can be used to predict stock market returns. Regressions and other econometric techniques can be used to forecast returns over any investment horizon (admittedly, they have fewer independent data points in long-horizon regressions). Thus, we can estimate a full term structure of expected returns. (Such forecasts are always model specific, but such a situation is no worse than the situation with informal and judgmental forecasts.)

The following empirical fact is worth emphasizing: Although beta risk has been well rewarded across asset classes (in the sense of the capital asset pricing model, in which the stock market, with a beta near 1, has outperformed the bond market, with a beta near 0, by 3–4 percent over long time periods), the same is not true *within* stock markets. High-beta and high-volatility assets in most stock markets have hardly outperformed their low-volatility peers in the long run; often, the reverse has occurred. Such risk without reward has increasingly attracted investor attention.

This paper focuses on the equity risk premium, but I want to finish with this exhortation: LOOK MORE BROADLY! A key theme in my recent book (Ilmanen 2011) is that relying exclusively or primarily on the ERP as the source of long-run returns causes portfolios to be inadequately diversified. Investors should broaden their horizons beyond asset class perspectives to consider various dynamic strategies (value, carry, trend, volatility, illiquidity) as well as underlying risk factors. The result for investors will be smarter portfolios than they currently have and better long-run performance.

REFERENCES

Allen, Franklin, and Roni Michaely. 2003. "Payout Policy." In *Handbook of the Economics of Finance*, vol. 1. 1st ed. Edited by George M. Constantinides, Milton Harris, and René M. Stulz. Amsterdam: Elsevier B.V.

Arnott, Robert D., and Peter L. Bernstein. 2002. "What Risk Premium Is 'Normal'?" *Financial Analysts Journal*, vol. 58, no. 2 (March/April):64–85.

Bernstein, William J., and Robert D. Arnott. 2003. "Earnings Growth: The Two Percent Dilution." *Financial Analysts Journal*, vol. 59, no. 5 (September/October):47–55.

Boudoukh, Jacob, Roni Michaely, Matthew Richardson, and Michael R. Roberts. 2007. "On the Importance of Measuring Payout Yield: Implications for Empirical Asset Pricing." *Journal of Finance*, vol. 62, no. 2 (April):877–915.

Campbell, John Y., and Robert J. Shiller. 1988. "Stock Prices, Earnings, and Expected Dividends." *Journal of Finance*, vol. 43, no. 3 (July):661–676.

Campbell, John Y., and Samuel B. Thompson. 2008. "Predicting Excess Stock Returns Out of Sample: Can Anything Beat the Historical Average?" *Review of Financial Studies*, vol. 21, no. 4 (July):1509–1531.

Cochrane, John. 2011. "Discount Rates." Presidential Address at the 2011 American Finance Association meeting (25 May); reprinted in *Journal of Finance*, vol. 66, no. 4 (August 2011):1047–1108 (http://faculty.chicagobooth.edu/john.cochrane/research/papers/AFA_pres_speech.pdf).

Cornell, Bradford. 2010. "Economic Growth and Equity Investing." *Financial Analysts Journal*, vol. 66, no. 1 (January/February):54–64.

Diermeier, Jeffrey J., Roger G. Ibbotson, and Laurence B. Siegel. 1984. "The Supply of Capital Market Returns." *Financial Analysts Journal*, vol. 40, no. 2 (March/April):74–80.

Dimson, Elroy, Paul Marsh, and Mike Staunton. 2002. *Triumph of the Optimists: 101 Years of Global Investment Returns*. Princeton, NJ: Princeton University Press.

———. 2011. *Credit Suisse Global Investment Returns Yearbook 2011*. Zurich: Credit Suisse Research Institute.

Fama, Eugene F., and Kenneth R. French. 2001. "Disappearing Dividends: Changing Firm Characteristics or Lower Propensity to Pay?" *Journal of Financial Economics*, vol. 60, no. 1 (April):3–43.

Ibbotson, Roger G., and Peng Chen. 2003. "Long-Run Stock Returns: Participating in the Real Economy." *Financial Analysts Journal*, vol. 59, no. 1 (January/February):88–98.

Ilmanen, Antti. 2011. *Expected Returns: An Investor's Guide to Harvesting Market Returns*. Chichester, U.K.: John Wiley & Sons.

MSCI Barra. 2010. "Is There a Link between GDP Growth and Equity Returns?" MSCI Barra Research Bulletin (May).

Welch, Ivo, and Amit Goyal. 2008. "A Comprehensive Look at the Empirical Performance of Equity Premium Prediction." *Review of Financial Studies*, vol. 21, no. 4 (July):1455–1508.

Will Bonds Outperform Stocks over the Long Run? Not Likely

Peng Chen, CFA
President, Global Investment Management Division
Morningstar Investment Management

Given the poor performance of stocks in the past decade, ample discussion has concerned the relative performance of stocks and bonds. Some even argue that investors should allocate assets entirely to bonds, not only because bonds are the safer investment but also because they believe bonds will outperform stocks over the long run. In other words, if bonds can deliver higher returns than stocks with less risk, why bother with stocks?

The impressive performance of the stock market in the 1980s and 1990s and the resulting rise in investor expectations spurred numerous articles that called attention to the historical market return and cautioned investors about overly optimistic expectations. Many studies forecasted equity returns that would be much lower when compared with the historical average. A few even predicted that stocks would not outperform bonds in the future. Later, after the bear markets of 2000–2002 and 2007–2009, the reverse happened. Investors tended to have very pessimistic expectations for stock returns. A study of the historical returns is, therefore, useful for bringing sense to either situation, whether overly optimistic or overly pessimistic expectations.

Table 1 shows the performance of the S&P 500 Index, the Barclays Capital (BarCap; formerly, Lehman Brothers) U.S. Aggregate Bond Index, the Ibbotson U.S. Intermediate-Term Government Bond Index, and the Ibbotson U.S. Long-Term Government Bond Index over various time periods. Average annual stock returns have been poor relative to bonds not just for the past 10 years; stock returns look mediocre for the past 20, 30, and even 40 years relative to bond returns. According to returns over the past 40 years, the argument that bonds might outperform stocks in the long run appears to be valid. But one should view these data with skepticism. Note that over the 20-, 30-, and 40-year periods, stocks actually performed quite well. In fact, stocks have outperformed their long-run average return since 1926. Only during the past 10 years have stocks significantly underperformed both the long-term average and bonds. We should also note that bonds over the past 40 years, in particular relative to stocks over the past 10, have done extremely well. Bonds have significantly outperformed their long-term averages since 1926.

Table 1. Compound Annualized Total Returns Ending December 2010

Span and Start Date	S&P 500	BarCap U.S. Aggregate	Ibbotson U.S. Intermediate-Term Government	Ibbotson U.S. Long-Term Government
1 Year: Jan 2010	15.06%	6.54%	7.12%	10.14%
5 Years: Jan 2006	2.29	5.80	6.06	5.58
10 Years: Jan 2001	1.41	5.84	5.64	6.64
20 Years: Jan 1991	9.14	6.89	6.56	8.44
30 Years: Jan 1981	10.71	8.92	8.51	10.18
40 Years: Jan 1971	10.14	8.32[a]	7.81	8.57
Jan 1926–Dec 2010	9.87	—	5.35	5.48

[a]The BarCap U.S. Aggregate goes back only to January 1976.

Over the very long term, however, it is no longer a contest. **Figure 1** shows the hypothetical value of $1 invested at the beginning of 1926 for the major capital market asset classes. Over this 85-year period, stocks easily beat bonds.

Consider these various long-term histories of U.S. stocks' compounded total returns:

January 1825–December 1925[1]	7.3%
January 1926–December 2010	9.9%
January 1825–December 2010	8.5%

The returns on the stock market have been consistently high for almost two centuries. The returns over the past 40 years are roughly comparable to the returns from the more distant past. Long-term history provides two major insights:

1. Stocks have outperformed bonds.
2. Stock returns are far more volatile than bond returns and are thus riskier. Given the additional amount of risk, it is not surprising that stocks do not outperform bonds in every period—even over extended periods of time.

Stocks vs. Bonds in the Future

How likely are stocks to outperform bonds in the future? As a first attempt to figure out the future, let's look in more detail at what happened during the past 40 years. We can decompose the stock and bond returns into several components:

Bond return = Current yield + Capital gain;

Stock return = Current yield + Earnings growth + P/E change.

Despite the substantial decline in yields over the past 40 years, and thus substantial capital gains on bonds, **Figure 2** shows that the bulk of returns on

[1]Stock returns for 1825–1925 are from Goetzmann, Ibbotson, and Peng (2001). For 1926–2010, returns are from Ibbotson Associates (2011).

Figure 1. Stocks, Bonds, Bills, and Inflation, 1926–2008
(lognormal)

1926 = $1.00

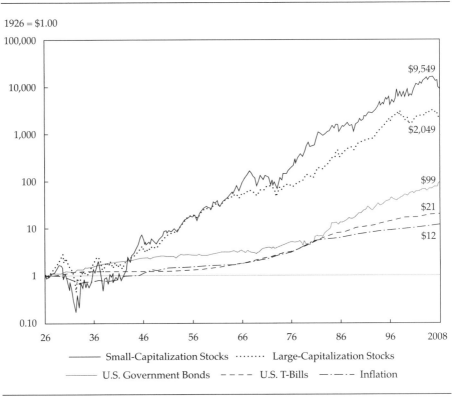

Note: Results assume reinvestment of income and no transaction costs or taxes.

the bond indices over the past 40 years came from the income return portion, or yield. On average, the bond income return from coupon payments was more than 7 percent. Capital gains caused by the yield decline made up the additional return. In contrast, over the past 40 years, stock returns consisted of 3.2 percent from dividend yield and 6.8 percent from capital gains. Next, let's look at what these components would look like going forward.

Today, bond yields are much lower than those shown in Figure 2. **Table 2** compares current bond yield information with yields at the beginning of 1971. As of the end of 2010, the Ibbotson long-term government bond yield was 4.14 percent and the Ibbotson intermediate-term government bond yield was only 1.70 percent. For bonds to continue to enjoy the same amount of capital gains over the next 40 years, their yields, especially the yield on intermediate-term government bonds, would probably have to move into negative territory. Such

119

Figure 2. Decomposition of Historical Returns, January 1971– December 2010

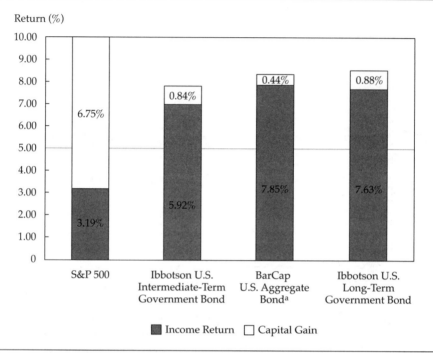

Return (%)

| | Income Return | ☐ Capital Gain |

aBarCap U.S. Aggregate goes back only to January 1976.

a development would be impossible because it implies that investors would be willing to pay for the privilege of lending their money to a borrower. Over the past 40 years, bond investors have enjoyed abundant returns because of a high-yield environment at the beginning of the period followed by a steady decline in yields. Going forward, these conditions are not likely to repeat; we are currently experiencing a much lower-yield environment with a higher likelihood of yield increases than decreases.

Table 2. Bond Yields

Bond Index	January 1971	December 2010	Change
Ibbotson U.S. Long-Term Government	6.12%	4.14%	−1.98
BarCap U.S. Aggregatea	7.92	2.97	−4.95
Ibbotson U.S. Intermediate-Term Government	5.70	1.70	−4.00

Note: Change is in percentage points.

aThe BarCap U.S. Aggregate goes back only to January 1976, so average yield was calculated as starting from that date.

Given the current low-yield environment, it would be almost impossible for bonds to generate the same amount of capital gains as they did in the past. In fact, a reasonable estimate might be that no more capital gains will be available in the near future because yields are at least as likely to rise as to fall.[2] If no future fall in yields were to occur, all of the return would have to come from the coupon return. That means the total return for bond investments would likely be 3–4 percent.

For stocks, the current dividend yield from January to December 2010 for the S&P 500 was 2.03 percent, which is a good baseline forecast of the future dividend yield levels. If stocks produce more than 2 percent in capital gains per year on average, adding the 2.03 percent dividend yield would result in a total stock return of 4 percent. Thus, just from simply looking at the decomposition of the past returns and making some simple forward-looking assumptions, one should expect that stocks will likely beat bonds going forward.

Let's elaborate some more on stocks' capital gains portion. Stocks' capital gain or price increase can be decomposed into nominal earnings growth and change in the P/E (see Ibbotson and Chen 2003). Historically, U.S. long-term nominal earnings growth has been roughly 4.65 percent, which is comparable to U.S. long-term nominal GDP growth. If we assumed that the market valuation level (the P/E of the S&P 500) would stay at the same level today over the next 40 years, then we would have an equity return of around 7 percent by adding the current dividend yield and nominal earnings growth. This means that the stock return will be in the 7 percent neighborhood, and the bond return will be around 3–4 percent. Even if we forecasted a decline in the valuation level, the 10-year average P/E would need to fall from its current level of about 20 to below 5 to result in average equity returns around 3 percent over the next 40 years. The lowest level of the P/E on the S&P 500 since 1926 was recorded at 7.1 in 1948; it has never gotten to a level less than 5, even through the Great Depression during the 1920s and 1930s and the 2008–09 global financial crisis. Again, this shows that it is unlikely that stocks will underperform bonds over the next 40 years.

Forecasting Expected Returns

The previous section showed a simple return decomposition and included some observations on future stock and bond returns. The following section will use the building block method to derive the expected returns on bonds and the supply-side equity risk premium model to derive expected returns on stocks.

---

[2]Some would even argue that bond yields are likely to increase over time, thus producing capital losses for bonds.

Building Block Method. The building block method was first introduced in Ibbotson and Sinquefield (1976). This approach uses current market yields as its foundation and adds estimated risk premiums to build expected return forecasts. This approach separates the expected return of each asset class into the three components shown in **Exhibit 1**.

Exhibit 1. Building Block Approach to Generating Expected Returns

Component	Description
Real risk-free rate	Return that can be earned without incurring any default or inflation risk
Expected inflation	Additional reward demanded to compensate investors for future price increases
Risk premium	Additional reward demanded for accepting uncertainty associated with a given asset class

When choosing a risk-free rate, Ibbotson Associates uses U.S. Treasury yield-curve rates with a maturity to match the investment period. **Table 3** outlines the risk-free rates that are applied to various time horizons. In this paper, because we are mostly interested in the long-term expected returns, we use the long-term (20-year) risk-free rate.

Table 3. Risk-Free Rates for Various Time Horizons

Time Horizon	Years to Maturity	Yield
Short term	5	2.01%
Intermediate term	10	3.30
Long term	20	4.13

Note: All data are from the U.S. Treasury Department website as reported for 31 December 2010.

Some risk premiums can be derived by subtracting the historical average return of one asset class from another or by subtracting the risk-free rate from the return of an asset class. In this way, past data are incorporated into the forecast of future returns; the assumptions are that the financial market is relatively efficient over time and that the realized return differential is a good measure of what investors are expecting to be compensated for in order to take on the various risk levels among different asset classes. Various premiums are added to the current risk-free rate to forecast the expected return unique to each asset class.

Historical returns are calculated over annual periods and may, depending on the nature of the benchmark, use income or total returns. In general, total returns are used for equity forecasts, whereas income returns are used for fixed-income forecasts. Total return is composed of capital appreciation and income (interest payments or dividends). For fixed-income asset classes, the realization of capital gains and losses is assumed to sum to zero over the time horizon of the investment. (In other words, coupon-paying bonds are assumed to be bought at par and are expected to mature at par.) The assumption is that the current market yield is the best forecast of *expected* returns on bonds (i.e., when investors buy bonds, they are expecting neither capital gain nor capital loss).

Expected Return for Bonds. For bond asset classes, Ibbotson Associates identifies three risk premiums that can impact the returns—a horizon premium, a default premium, and a mortgage prepayment premium, as shown in **Table 4.** The horizon premium measures the excess yield that investors in long-term fixed income expect to receive in exchange for accepting additional uncertainty and potential loss of liquidity. Ibbotson Associates estimates the horizon premium as the difference (in the income return) between two government bonds. The first government bond (which is called the "government bond proxy") has the same maturity as the asset class being modeled; the second government bond is the risk-free rate.

Table 4. Detailed Methodology on Expected Return Estimations, 31 December 2010

Benchmark	Expected Return, Geometric	Long-Term Risk-Free Rate	Equity Risk Premium	Fixed Income		
				Horizon Premium	Corporate Default Premium	Mortgage Prepayment Premium
Stocks (S&P 500)	7.61%	4.13%	3.34%			
BarCap U.S. Aggregate	4.45	4.13	—	−0.34%	0.26%	0.40%
Ibbotson U.S. Long-Term Government	4.13	4.13	—	—	—	—
Ibbotson U.S. Intermediate-Term Government	3.61	4.13	—	−0.52	—	—
T-bills	2.49	4.13	—	−1.64	—	—

The corporate default premium measures the historical reward received for holding corporate bonds rather than government bonds of the same maturity. The corporate default premium is equal to the difference between a pure corporate benchmark and a government bond of the same maturity. This difference is multiplied by the corporate exposure in the particular bond asset class.

The mortgage prepayment premium depends on early delivery of mortgage payments that may subsequently change the cash flow and total return received by an investor. The premium is calculated as the difference between the arithmetic mean income return of an index of pure mortgage-backed securities and the arithmetic mean income return of a government bond proxy with the same maturity as the mortgage-backed index. This difference is then multiplied by the percentage of mortgage exposure found in the asset class benchmark:

The specific fixed-income-premium calculations are as follows:

Horizon premium =	Ibbotson government bond proxy[a] income return	−	Ibbotson government bond proxy[b] income return	
Corporate default premium	= Corporate bond index income return	−	Ibbotson government bond proxy[a] income return	× Percent corporate bond exposure
Mortgage prepayment premium	= Mortgage bond index income return	−	Ibbotson government bond proxy[a] income return	× Percent mortgage bond exposure

[a]Same maturity (average or current) as the asset class benchmark.
[b]Same maturity as the time horizon (i.e., 20 years).

The resulting estimated expected returns for various bond asset classes are shown in Table 4.

Long-Term Expected Return for Stocks and Equity Risk Premium. The expected return of stocks over bonds has been estimated by a number of authors using various approaches. Such studies can be categorized into four groups based on the approaches they have taken. The first group of studies derives the ERP from historical returns between stocks and bonds. By taking the long-term bond returns (5.48 percent) from the stock returns (9.87 percent) from Table 1, we arrive at a historical compounded equity risk premium estimate of 4.16 percent. The second group uses supply-side models to measure the expected ERP. These models incorporate fundamental information, such as earnings, dividends, and overall productivity. A third group adopts demand-side models that derive the expected return of equities through the payoff demanded by equity investors for bearing additional risk. The fourth group relies on the opinions of financial professionals through broad surveys.

Ibbotson Associates establishes an equity risk premium by following the supply-side approach outlined in Ibbotson and Chen (2003). Their work combined the first and second approaches to arrive at a forecast of the ERP. By proposing a new supply-side methodology, the Ibbotson–Chen study challenges current arguments that future returns on stocks over bonds will be negative or close to zero. The results affirm the relationship between the stock market and the overall economy. They also provide implications for investors creating a policy for allocating assets between stocks and bonds. The following section will briefly explain the methodology presented in Ibbotson and Chen (2003). For detailed explanations, please refer to the original article.

■ *Supply model.* Long-term expected equity returns can be forecasted by using supply-side models. The supply of stock market returns is generated by the productivity of corporations in the real economy. Investors should not expect a much higher or lower return than that produced by the companies in the real economy. Thus, over the long run, equity returns should be close to the long-run supply estimate.

Earnings, dividends, and capital gains are supplied by corporate profitability. **Figure 3** illustrates that earnings and dividends have historically grown in tandem with the overall economy (GDP per capita), adjusting for inflation. So, if one assumes that the economy will continue to grow, dividends and earnings should also continue to grow, thus continuing to drive stock performance. Capital gains did not, however, outpace the stock market—primarily because the P/E increased by a factor of 2 during the same period. In other words, investors' appetite to pay for per unit of earnings has increased roughly two times over the period.

Figure 3. Growth of $1.00 in GDP per Capita, Earnings, and Dividends, 31 December 1925 to December 2010

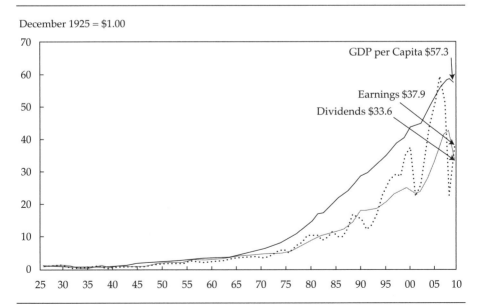

■ *Forward-looking earnings model.* Two main components make up the supply of equity returns: current returns in the form of dividends and long-term productivity growth in the form of capital gains. The discussion that follows identifies and analyzes components of the earnings model that are tied to the supply of equity returns. This discussion leads to an estimate of the long-term sustainable equity return based on historical information about the supply components.

The Ibbotson Associates earnings model breaks the historical equity return into four components. Only three—inflation, income return, and growth in real earnings per share—have historically been supplied by companies. The growth in P/Es, the fourth piece, is a reflection of investors' increased appetite to pay the price per unit of earnings produced. We believe that the past supply of corporate growth (through dividend and earnings growth) is forecasted to continue but that a continued increase in investors' appetite to pay for per unit of earnings is not. The P/E rose dramatically over the past 80 years because investors believed that corporate earnings would grow faster in the future. This growth in P/E accounted for a small portion of the total return on equities during the period. **Figure 4** depicts the P/E from 1926 to 2009. The P/E was 10.22 at the beginning of 1926 and 20.61 in 2009—an average increase of 0.84 percent

Figure 4. P/E, 1926–2009

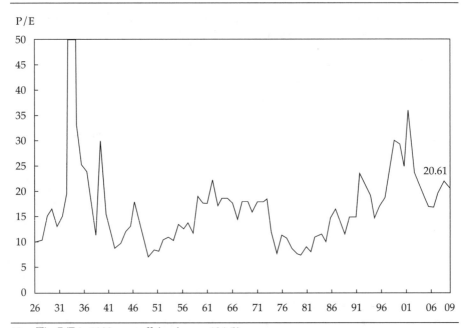

Note: The P/E in 1932 went off the chart to 136.50.

per year. The highest P/E was 136.50, recorded in 1932, and the lowest was 7.07, recorded in 1948. (The P/Es in Figure 4 may differ from some of the others presented in this book because of varying definitions of earnings.)

Ibbotson Associates subtracts the historical P/E growth rate from the equity risk premium forecast because we do not believe that the P/E will continue to increase in the future. The market serves as the cue. The current P/E is the market's best guess regarding the future of corporate earnings, and we have no reason to believe, at this time, that the market will change its mind. Thus, the supply of equity return includes only inflation, the growth in real EPS, and income return. Instead of using one-year earnings in calculating the P/E, as in Ibbotson and Chen (2003), we use three-year average earnings in this calculation. The reason is that reported earnings are affected not only by long-term productivity but also by "one-time" items that do not necessarily have the same consistent impact year after year.[3] For example, the 2003 earnings used in this calculation are the average reported earnings from 2002, 2003, and 2004. For 2009, the earnings are the average of reported earnings in 2008 and 2009 and the estimated earnings for 2010. Using a three-year average rather than year-by-year numbers is more reflective of the long-term trend.

The historical P/E expansion is calculated to be roughly 0.82 percent per year; therefore, by subtracting the 0.82 percent from the 4.16 percent historical equity risk premium estimate, we obtain the forward-looking equity risk premium estimate of 3.34 percent. Adding this ERP estimate to the 4.13 percent bond yield, we estimate the forward-looking equity nominal compounded return to be 7.61 percent. In other words, we expect stocks to beat bonds by 3.34 percent per year over the next 20 years.

At the end of 2010, the 20-year Treasury inflation index yield was 1.64 percent, the nominal 20-year bond yield was 4.13 percent, and expected inflation was 2.45 percent. Therefore, the forecasted real stock return is 5.04 percent—again outperforming the forecasted real bond return of 1.64 percent by 3.34 percent compounded per year. The final results are presented in Table 4 and **Table 5**.

Implications for the Investor

For the long-term investor, asset allocation is the primary determinant of the variability of returns. Of all the decisions investors make, therefore, the asset allocation decision is the most important.

---

[3]Effective March 2009, Ibbotson Associates began using a blend of operating and reporting earnings for the period 1988 to the present when calculating P/Es. This approach mitigates the impact of severe write-downs of reported earnings and the resulting P/Es.

Table 5. Expected Return (20-Year Horizon), 31 December 2010

Benchmark	Geometric Return	Standard Deviation
Stocks (S&P 500)	7.61%	20.39%
BarCap U.S. Aggregate	4.45	6.59
Ibbotson U.S. Long-Term Government	4.13	11.73
Ibbotson U.S. Intermediate-Term Government	3.61	6.59
T-bills	2.49	3.43

The most important asset allocation decision is the allocation between stocks and bonds. Thus, the expected return between stocks and bonds, or the equity risk premium, is the most important number. A negative ERP implies that the investor should favor allocations to fixed income, whereas a positive ERP indicates an allocation to equities. (Of course, in addition to the ERP, the investor's risk tolerance, investment goals, time horizon, etc., need to be considered.) Therefore, the asset allocation decision is only as good as the accuracy of the investor's forecast of the expected equity risk premium.

Ibbotson Associates believes that stocks will continue to provide significant returns over the long run. We calculate the geometric, or the compounded, ERP based on applying the supply-side earnings model with three-year average earnings to be 3.34 percent—82 bps lower than the straight historical estimate. This forecast for the market is in line with both the historical supply measures of public corporations (i.e., earnings) and overall economic productivity (GDP per capita).

Conclusion

Not only have bonds outperformed stocks over various recent periods because of the financial crisis, but they also have roughly matched stock performance over the past 40 years. This fact raises the question, will bonds continue to outperform stocks?

This paper demonstrated that a close examination of history shows that stock returns over the last 40 years were virtually in line with the long-term historical average. Bond returns, however, were not only much higher than their historical averages but also higher than their current yields. This high bond return is the result of high interest rates in the 1970s and a subsequent declining interest rate environment. Given today's low-interest-rate environment, this scenario for bonds is very unlikely to repeat itself in the future. Investors hoping that bonds will outperform stocks in the coming years are likely to be disappointed.

Stocks tend to outperform bonds over time but are much riskier, even over longer periods. Bonds can outperform stocks over a long period, but investors need almost perfect timing to get in and out of the market to realize such returns. Ibbotson Associates believes the right strategy is to follow a disciplined asset allocation policy that considers the return–risk trade-offs by taking advantage of the diversification benefits over time provided by investing in both stocks and bonds.

Ibbotson Associates, Inc., is a registered investment advisor and wholly owned subsidiary of Morningstar, Inc. The Ibbotson name and logo are either trademarks or service marks of Ibbotson Associates, Inc. The information contained in this document is for informational purposes only and is the proprietary material of Ibbotson Associates. Reproduction, transcription, or other use, by any means, in whole or in part, without the prior written consent of Ibbotson, is prohibited. Opinions expressed are as of the current date; such opinions are subject to change without notice. Ibbotson Associates, Inc., shall not be responsible for any trading decisions, damages, or other losses resulting from, or related to, the information, data, analyses or opinions or their use.

REFERENCES

Goetzmann, William N., Roger G. Ibbotson, and Liang Peng. 2001. "A New Historical Database for the NYSE 1815 to 1925: Performance and Predictability." *Journal of Financial Markets*, vol. 4, no. 1 (January):1–32.

Ibbotson Associates. 2011. *Stocks, Bonds, Bills, and Inflation 2010 Yearbook*. Chicago: Ibbotson Associates.

Ibbotson, Roger G., and Peng Chen. 2003. "Long-Run Stock Returns: Participating in the Real Economy." *Financial Analysts Journal*, vol. 59, no. 1 (January/February):88–98.

Ibbotson, Roger G., and Rex A. Sinquefield. 1976. "Stocks, Bonds, Bills, and Inflation: Simulations of the Future (1976–2000)." *Journal of Business*, vol. 49, no. 3 (July):313–338.

Price-to-Earnings Ratios: Growth and Discount Rates

Andrew Ang
Ann F. Kaplan Professor of Business
Columbia University

Xiaoyan Zhang
Associate Professor of Finance
Krannert School of Management, Purdue University

In a present-value model, movements in price-to-earnings ratios must reflect variations in discount rates (which embed risk premiums) and growth opportunities (which involve the cash flow and earnings-generating capacity of the firm's investments).[1] We decomposed P/Es into a no-growth value, defined to be the perpetuity value of future earnings that are held constant with full payout of earnings, and the present value of growth opportunities (PVGO), which is the value of the stock in excess of the no-growth value. To accomplish this decomposition, we used a dynamic model that accounts for time-varying risk premiums and stochastic growth opportunities.

An important aspect of our work is that we took into account a stochastic investment opportunity set with time-varying growth and discount rates. P/Es can be high not only when growth opportunities are perceived to be favorable but also when expected returns are low. For example, during the late 1990s and early 2000s, P/Es were very high. The cause might have been high prices incorporating large growth opportunities, but Jagannathan, McGrattan, and Scherbina (2000) and Claus and Thomas (2001), among others, have argued that during this time, discount rates were low. In contrast to our no-growth and PVGO decompositions, in which both discount rates and growth rates are stochastic, in the standard decompositions of no-growth and PVGO components, discount rates and growth rates are constant. Other standard analyses in the industry, such as the ratio of the P/E to growth (often called the "PEG ratio"), implicitly assign all variations in P/Es to growth opportunities because the analyses do not allow for time-varying discount rates.

---

[1]This approach decomposes the value of a firm into the value of its assets in place plus real options (or growth opportunities). This decomposition was recognized as early as Miller and Modigliani (1961).

Static Case

An instructive approach is to consider first the standard decomposition of the P/E into the no-growth and growth components that is typically done in an MBA-level finance class. The exposition here is adapted from Bodie, Kane, and Marcus (2009, p. 597).

Suppose earnings grow at rate g, the discount rate is δ, and the payout ratio is denoted by po. The value of equity, P, is then given by

$$P = \frac{EA \times po}{\delta - g}, \tag{1}$$

where EA is expected earnings next year. The P/E—that is, $P/E = P/EA$—is then simply

$$\begin{aligned} P/E &= \frac{P}{EA} \\ &= \frac{po}{\delta - g}. \end{aligned} \tag{2}$$

We can decompose market value P into a no-growth component and a growth component. The growth component is considered to be the PVGO. The no-growth value, P^{ng}, is defined as the present value of future earnings with no growth (so, $g = 0$ and $po = 1$):

$$P^{ng} = \frac{EA}{\delta}. \tag{3}$$

The growth component is defined as the remainder:

$$\begin{aligned} PVGO &= \frac{EA \times po}{\delta - g} - \frac{EA}{\delta} \\ &= \frac{EA\left[g - (1 - po)\delta\right]}{\delta(\delta - g)}, \end{aligned} \tag{4}$$

and the two sum up to the total market value:

$$P = P^{ng} + PVGO. \tag{5}$$

The decomposition of firm value into no-growth and PVGO components is important because, by definition, the no-growth component involves only discount rates whereas the PVGO component involves both the discount rate and the effects of cash flow growth. Understanding which component dominates gives insight into what drives P/Es. The static case cannot be used to decompose P/Es into no-growth and PVGO values over time, however, because it assumes that earnings growth (g), discount rates (δ), and payout ratios (po) remain constant over time. Clearly, this assumption is not true. Thus, to examine the no-growth and PVGO values of P/Es, we need to build a dynamic model.

The Dynamic Model

We made two changes to the static case to handle time-varying investment opportunities. First, we put "t" subscripts on the variables to indicate that they change over time. Second, for analytical tractability, we worked in log returns, log growth rates, and log payout ratios.

We defined the discount rate, δ_t, as

$$\delta_t = \ln E_t \left(\frac{P_{t+1} + D_{t+1}}{P_t} \right), \tag{6}$$

where P_t is the equity price at time t and D_t is the dividend at time t. Earnings growth is defined as

$$g_t = \ln \left(\frac{EA_t}{EA_{t-1}} \right), \tag{7}$$

where EA_t is earnings at time t. Finally, the log payout ratio at time t is

$$po_t = \ln \left(\frac{D_t}{EA_t} \right). \tag{8}$$

In this notation, if $\delta_t = \bar{\delta}$, $g_t = \bar{g}$, and $po_t = \overline{po}$ are all constant, then the familiar P/E in Equation 2 written in simple growth rates or returns becomes

$$\frac{P}{EA} = \frac{\exp\left(\overline{po}\right)}{\exp\left(\bar{\delta} - \bar{g}\right) - 1}. \tag{9}$$

Factors. We specified factors X_t that drive P/Es. The first three factors in X_t are the risk-free rate, r_t^f; the earnings growth rate, g_t; and the payout ratio, po_t. We included two other variables that predict returns: the growth rate of industrial production, ip_t, and term spreads, $term_t$. We selected these variables after considering variables that, on their own, forecast total returns, earnings growth, or both. We also included a latent factor, f_t, that captures variation in expected returns not accounted for by the observable factors. We specified latent factor f_t to be orthogonal to the other factors. Thus, $X_t = (r_t^f \; g_t \; po_t \; ip_t \; term_t \; f_t)'$.

We assumed that state variables X_t follow a vector autoregression (VAR) with one lag:

$$X_{t+1} = \mu + \Phi X_t + \Sigma \varepsilon_{t+1}, \tag{10}$$

where ε_t follows a standard normal distribution with zero mean and unit standard deviation. The companion form, Φ, allows earnings growth and payout ratios to be predictable by both past earnings growth and payout ratios and other macro variables.

The long-run risk model of Bansal and Yaron (2004) incorporates a highly persistent factor in the conditional mean of cash flows. Our model accomplishes the same effect by including persistent variables in X_t, especially the risk-free rate and payout ratio, which are both highly autocorrelated.

To complete the model, we assumed that discount rates δ_t are a linear function of state variables X_t:

$$\delta_t = \delta_0 + \boldsymbol{\delta}_1' X_t. \tag{11}$$

Equation 11 subsumes the special cases of constant total expected returns by setting $\delta_1 = 0$ and subsumes the general case of time-varying discount rates when $\delta_1 \neq 0$. Because f_t is latent, we placed a unit coefficient in δ_1 that corresponds to f_t for identification.

The Dynamic P/E. Under the assumptions shown in Equation 10 and Equation 11, the dynamic P/E can be written as

$$P/E_t = \sum_{i=1}^{\infty} \exp\left(a_i + \boldsymbol{b}_i' X_t\right). \tag{12}$$

The coefficients a_i and b_i are given in Appendix A.[2]

Our model of the P/E belongs to the asset-pricing literature that builds dynamic valuation models. The approaches of Campbell and Shiller (1988) and Vuolteenaho (2002) to model the price/dividend ratio (P/D) and the P/E, respectively, require log-linearization assumptions. In contrast, our model produces analytically tractable solutions for P/Es. Recently, Bekaert, Engstrom, and Grenadier (2010) and van Binsbergen and Koijen (2010) examined dynamic P/Ds, but not P/Es, in models with closed-form solutions. Our model is more closely related to the analytical dynamic earnings models of Ang and Liu (2001) and Bakshi and Chen (2005), in which cash flows are predictable and discount rates vary over time. Ang and Liu, however, modeled price-to-book ratios instead of P/Es, and Bakshi and Chen's model of the P/E requires the payout ratio to be constant.

Growth and No-Growth Components. The no-growth P/E can be interpreted as a perpetuity, where at each time, a unit cash flow is discounted by the cumulated market discount rates prevailing up until that time. In the full P/E in Equation 12, growth occurs by plowing earnings back into the firm. In the no-growth P/E, earnings are fully paid out; consequently, the payout ratio

---

[2]A full derivation is available in the online appendix at www.columbia.edu/~aa610.

does not directly influence the no-growth P/E value. The payout ratio is relevant in the no-growth P/E, however, because the payout ratio is a state variable and its dynamics are allowed to influence future earnings through the VAR process.

The no-growth P/E, P/E_t^{ng}, where earnings growth is everywhere 0 and the payout ratio is equal to 1, can be written as

$$P/E_t^{ng} = \sum_{i=1}^{\infty} \exp\left(a_i^* + b_i^{*'} X_t\right), \tag{13}$$

where a_i^* and b_i^* are given in Appendix A.

The present value of growth opportunities is defined as the difference between the P/E, which incorporates growth, and the no-growth P/E:

$$P/E_t = P/E_t^{ng} + PVGO_t. \tag{14}$$

Empirical Results

We used data on dividend yields, P/Es, price returns (capital gains only), and total returns (capital gains and dividends) on the S&P 500 Index from the first quarter (Q1) of 1953 to the fourth quarter (Q4) of 2009.

Panel A of **Figure 1** plots the log index of the S&P 500 Total Return Index across our sample. The decline during the mid-1970s recession, the strong bull market of the 1990s, the decline after the technology bubble in the early 2000s, and the drop resulting from the 2008–09 financial crisis are clearly visible. Panel B graphs the P/E, which averages 18.5 over the sample period. The P/E suddenly increased in Q4:2008 to 60.7 and reached a peak of 122 in Q2:2009. In Q4:2009, the P/E came down to 21.9. The large increase in the P/E from Q4:2008 through Q3:2009 is the result of large, negative reported earnings in Q4:2008 during the financial crisis. This development caused the moving four-quarter average of earnings to sharply decrease. While prices were declining during the financial crisis, an even greater decrease was occurring in reported earnings, which caused the increase in the P/E. Panel C of Figure 1 reports S&P 500 dividend yields, which reached a low at the end of the bull market in 2000.

Estimation Results. **Table 1** reports the parameter estimates of the model. The two most significant predictors of the discount rate are earnings growth, g, with a coefficient of 0.38, and the growth rate of industrial production, ip, with a coefficient of -1.28. The estimated VAR parameters show that all factors are highly persistent, and this persistence dominates: No other factor except the variables themselves Granger-causes risk-free rates, earnings growth, or payout ratios.[3]

---

[3] Estimation of the model is discussed in the online appendix at www.columbia.edu/~aa610.

Figure 1. Log Index Levels, Payout Ratios, and Dividend Yields for S&P 500 Total Return Index, Q1:1953–Q4:2009

A. Log of the Index Level

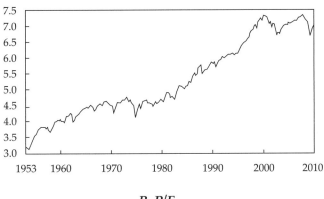

B. P/E

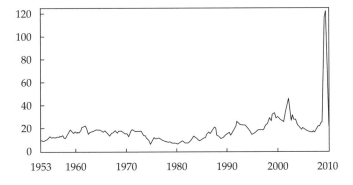

C. Dividend Yield

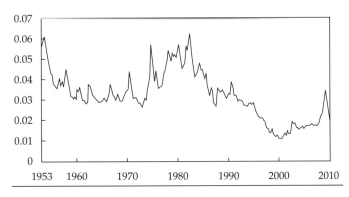

Table 1. Parameter Estimates
(*p*-values in parentheses)

	rf	g	po	ip	$term$	f
Discount rate parameters δ_1:	0.325	0.381	0.164	−1.283	1.203	1
	(0.775)	(0.121)	(0.088)	(0.238)	(1.728)	—
VAR parameter Φ						
rf	0.863	0.26	0.012	−0.005	0.088	0
	(0.089)	(0.008)	(0.012)	(0.033)	(0.191)	—
g	0.917	0.628	0.650	0.115	3.677	0
	(1.385)	(0.353)	(0.426)	(0.362)	(3.446)	—
po	−0.771	−0.514	0.303	0.045	−2.805	0
	(1.292)	(0.328)	(0.415)	(0.360)	(3.131)	—
ip	−0.244	0.096	0.071	−0.169	0.908	0
	(0.237)	(0.057)	(0.041)	(0.108)	(0.737)	—
$term$	0.021	−0.017	−0.003	−0.025	0.502	0
	(0.036)	(0.005)	(0.007)	(0.019)	(0.092)	—
f	0	0	0	0	0	0.904
	—	—	—	—	—	(0.003)

We plotted the estimated discount rates in **Figure 2**. The full discount rate (solid line) is overlaid with the implied discount rate without the latent factor, f_t (dotted line). The two discount rates have a correlation of 0.91. Thus, the observable factors capture most of the variation in expected returns. Without the latent factor, the observable factors $z_t = (rf_t\ g_t\ po_t\ ip_t\ term_t)$ account for 18.0 percent of the variance of total returns; adding the latent factor brings the proportion up to 27.5 percent.

Figure 2 shows that discount rates declined noticeably in the 1990s—from 14.5 percent in Q1:1991 to −14.5 percent in Q1:2002. The −14.5 percent corresponds to what was at that time the all-time-high P/E in the sample, 46.5. The latent factor was very negative during this time; the model explains the high P/E as coming from low discount rates. Recently, during the financial crisis, discount rates were again negative. For example, in Q4:2008, the discount rate was −16.3 percent. Q4:2008 was characterized by pronounced negative reported earnings. The P/E increased to 60.7 at this time because of the low earnings relative to market values. The model again explains the high P/E by the low discount rate. The low discount rates at this time were caused by the large decrease in earnings growth. Subsequent returns over the 2008–09 period were indeed extremely low.

Figure 2. Discount Rates, Q1:1953–Q4:2009

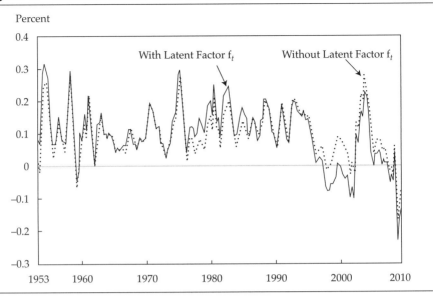

Drivers of the P/E. In Table 2, we report variance decompositions of the P/E. We computed the variance of the P/E implied by the model through the sample, where the factor z was held constant at its unconditional mean, $var_z(P/E)$. The variance decomposition resulting from factor z is given by $1 - var_z(P/E)/var(P/E)$, where $var(P/E)$ is the variance of the P/E in the data. These decompositions do not sum to 1.0 because the factors are correlated. Table 2 shows that the macro variables play a large role in explaining the dynamics of P/Es. Risk-free rates, earnings growth, and payout ratios explain, respectively, 18 percent, 38 percent, and 66 percent of the variance of P/Es.

Table 2. Variance Decompositions of the P/E

Parameter	Variance Explained
rf	17.8%
g	38.3
po	65.9
ip	−38.6
$term$	7.5
f	70.5

The variance attribution for growth in industrial production is negative because diminished industrial production results in more volatile discount rates and greater volatility of P/Es. The latent factor, f, plays an important role in matching P/Es, with a variance attribution of 71 percent. This finding is consistent with Figure 2, where some occasionally pronounced differences are visible between discount rates produced only with macro variables and discount rates estimated with the latent factor.

Growth and No-Growth Decompositions. Figure 3 plots the no-growth components together with the P/E. Most of the variation in the P/E is a result of growth components. The average no-growth P/E defined in Equation 13 is 3.8, compared with an average P/E in the data of 18.5. Thus, no-growth components account for, on average, 20.7 percent of the P/E; most of the total P/E is a result of the PVGO. The no-growth component is remarkably constant (as is clearly shown in Figure 3) and has a volatility of 0.853, compared with a volatility of 12.7 for the P/E. A variance decomposition of the P/E is

$$\mathrm{var}\left(P/E_t\right) = \mathrm{var}\left(P/E_t^{ng}\right) + \mathrm{var}\left(PVGO_t\right) + 2\,\mathrm{cov}\left(P/E_t^{ng}, PVGO_t\right). \qquad (15)$$

$$\underset{100\%}{} \quad \underset{0.5\%}{} \quad \underset{94.8\%}{} \quad \underset{4.7\%}{}$$

Thus, 95 percent of P/E variation is explained by growth components, or the PVGO term. The perpetuity value of no-growth is relatively constant because discount rates are highly mean reverting: The year-on-year autocorrelation of discount rates over the sample is 0.34. Thus, the discounted earnings in the no-growth P/E rapidly revert to their long-term average.

Figure 3. No-Growth and Growth Components of the P/E, Q1:1953–Q4:2009

In **Table 3**, we report various correlations of the no-growth and PVGO P/Es. The no-growth and PVGO components have a correlation of 0.363, but this correlation has only a small effect on total P/E variation because of the low volatility of no-growth P/E values. Thus, most of the variation in the total P/E is caused by growth opportunities, and not surprisingly, the PVGO P/E and the total P/E are highly correlated, at 0.998. Both the growth P/E and the total P/E decrease when risk-free rates and earnings growth increase. The correlation of the total P/E with earnings growth is particularly strong at −0.766. High earnings growth by itself increases earnings, which is the denominator of the P/E, and causes P/Es to decrease, resulting in the high negative correlation between earnings growth and the P/E. But another discount rate effect occurs because high earnings growth causes discount rates to significantly increase (see Table 1). This effect also causes P/Es to decrease. High payout ratios, as expected, are positively correlated with the P/E at 0.713. Finally, the latent factor, f, is negatively correlated with the P/E because it is only a discount rate factor: By construction, P/Es are high when f is low.

Table 3. Correlation of Growth (PVGO) and No-Growth Components of the P/E

	No Growth P/E	PVGO P/E
PVGO P/E:	0.363	
Data P/E:	0.421	0.998
rf	−0.353	−0.426
g	−0.051	−0.766
po	−0.292	0.713
ip	0.114	−0.303
$term$	0.027	0.390
f	−0.903	−0.538

Conclusion

We decomposed the P/E into a no-growth component (the perpetuity value of future earnings held constant with full payout) and a component termed PVGO that reflects the growth opportunities and real options a firm has to invest in the future. We valued both components in a dynamic stochastic environment where risk premiums and earnings growth are stochastic. We found that discount rates exhibit significant variation: 27.5 percent of the variation in total returns is caused by persistent, time-varying expected return components. However, although the variation of discount rates is large, these rates are highly mean reverting. The result is that the no-growth value of earnings exhibits relatively little volatility. The PVGO component dominates; it accounts for the bulk of the level and variation of P/Es in the data: Approximately 80 percent of the level and 95 percent of the variance of P/Es are a result of time-varying growth opportunities.

We thank Geert Bekaert, Sigbjørn Berg, and Tørres Trovik for helpful discussions.

Appendix A

Here, we provide the coefficients a_i and b_i and the definition of the P/E as used by the S&P 500. All the formulas are derived in the online appendix at www.columbia.edu/~aa610.

Full and No-Growth P/Es. The coefficients a_i and b_i for the P/E in Equation 12 are given by

$$a_{i+1} = -\delta_0 + a_i + \left(\mathbf{e}_2 + \boldsymbol{b}_i\right)' \boldsymbol{\mu} + \frac{1}{2}\left(\mathbf{e}_2 + \boldsymbol{b}_i\right)' \Sigma\Sigma'\left(\mathbf{e}_2 + \boldsymbol{b}_i\right)$$

and

$$b_i = -\boldsymbol{\delta}_1 + \Phi'\left(\mathbf{e}_2 + \boldsymbol{b}_i\right),$$

where $\mathbf{e}_n$ is a vector of 0s with a 1 in the nth position. The initial conditions are

$$a_1 = -\delta_0 + \left(\mathbf{e}_2 + \mathbf{e}_3\right)' \boldsymbol{\mu} + \frac{1}{2}\left(\mathbf{e}_2 + \mathbf{e}_3\right)' \Sigma\Sigma'\left(\mathbf{e}_2 + \mathbf{e}_3\right)$$

and

$$b_1 = -\boldsymbol{\delta}_1 + \Phi'\left(\mathbf{e}_2 + \mathbf{e}_3\right).$$

The coefficients in the no-growth P/E, P/E_t^{ng}, in Equation 13 are given by

$$a_{i+1}^* = -\delta_0 + a_i^* + \boldsymbol{b}_i^{*'}\boldsymbol{\mu} + \frac{1}{2}\boldsymbol{b}_i^{*'}\Sigma\Sigma'\boldsymbol{b}_i^*$$

and

$$b_{i+1}^* = -\boldsymbol{\delta}_1 + \Phi'\boldsymbol{b}_i^*,$$

where a_i^* and b_i^* have initial values $a_i^* = -\delta_0$ and $b_i^* = -\boldsymbol{\delta}_1$.

Data. The P/E defined by Standard & Poor's is the market value at time t divided by trailing 12-month earnings reported from t to $t - 1$. To back out earnings growth from P/Es, we used the following transformation:

$$\exp\left(g_{t+1}\right) = \frac{EA_{t+1}}{EA_t}$$

$$= \left(\frac{P/E_t}{P/E_{t+1}}\right)\left(\frac{P_{t+1}}{P_t}\right),$$

where P_{t+1}/P_t is the price gain (capital gain) on the market from t to $t +1$.

The dividend yield reported by Standard & Poor's is also constructed from trailing 12-month summed dividends. We computed the log payout ratio from the ratio of the dividend yield, $dy_t = D_t/P_t$, to the inverse P/E:

$$\exp\left(po_t\right) = \frac{dy_t}{1/\left(P/E\right)_t}$$

$$= \frac{D_t}{EA_t}.$$

For the risk-free rate, r_t^f, we used one-year zero-coupon yields expressed as a log return, which we obtained from the Fama Files derived from the CRSP U.S. Government Bond Files. For the macro variables, we expressed industrial production growth, ip, as a log year-on-year growth rate for which we used the industrial production index from the St. Louis Federal Reserve. We defined the term spread, *term*, as the difference in annual yields between 10-year and 1-year government bonds, which we obtained from CRSP.

BIBLIOGRAPHY

Ang, A., and J. Liu. 2001. "A General Affine Earnings Valuation Model." *Review of Accounting Studies*, vol. 6, no. 4 (December):397–425.

Bakshi, G., and Z. Chen. 2005. "Stock Valuation in Dynamic Economies." *Journal of Financial Markets*, vol. 8, no. 2 (May):115–151.

Bansal, R., and A. Yaron. 2004. "Risk for the Long Run: A Potential Resolution of Asset Pricing Puzzles." *Journal of Finance*, vol. 59, no. 4 (August):1481–1509.

Bekaert, G., E. Engstrom, and S.R. Grenadier. 2010. "Stock and Bond Returns with Moody Investors." *Journal of Empirical Finance*, vol. 17, no. 5 (December):867–894.

Bodie, Z., A. Kane, and A.J. Marcus. 2009. *Investments*. 8th ed. New York: McGraw-Hill/Irwin.

Campbell, J.Y., and R.J. Shiller. 1988. "The Dividend-Price Ratio and Expectations of Future Dividends and Discount Factors." *Review of Financial Studies*, vol. 1, no. 3 (July):195–228.

Claus, J., and J. Thomas. 2001. "Equity Premia as Low as Three Percent? Evidence from Analysts' Earnings Forecasts for Domestic and International Stock Markets." *Journal of Finance*, vol. 56, no. 5 (October):1629–1666.

Fama, E.F., and K.R. French. 2002. "The Equity Premium." *Journal of Finance*, vol. 57, no. 2 (April):637–659.

Jagannathan, R., E.R. McGrattan, and A. Scherbina. 2000. "The Declining U.S. Equity Premium." *Federal Reserve Bank of Minneapolis Quarterly Review*, vol. 24, no. 4 (Fall):3–19.

Miller, M.H., and F. Modigliani. 1961. "Dividend Policy, Growth, and the Valuation of Shares." *Journal of Business*, vol. 34, no. 4 (October):411–433.

van Binsbergen, J., and R.S.J. Koijen. 2010. "Predictive Regressions: A Present-Value Approach." *Journal of Finance*, vol. 65, no. 4 (August):1439–1471.

Vuolteenaho, T. 2002. "What Drives Firm-Level Stock Returns?" *Journal of Finance*, vol. 51, no. 1 (February):233–264.

Long-Term Stock Returns Unshaken by Bear Markets

Jeremy J. Siegel
Russell E. Palmer Professor of Finance
Wharton School of the University of Pennsylvania

The first Equity Risk Premium Forum, sponsored by CFA Institute, was held on 8 November 2001, not long after the September 11 terrorist attacks and coincident with the first of two devastating bear markets in the first decade of the new millennium. At the time of the first forum, stocks had already fallen by more than half of what would become a nearly 50 percent decline from the peak reached in March 2000 to the low in October 2002. Over the four years after the low, the equity market recovered all of its losses and moved into new all-time-high territory. But the 2008 financial crisis precipitated a more severe bear market than 2000–2002 and the worst since the Great Crash of 1929–1932. In the financial crisis, the S&P 500 Index plunged 57 percent from October 2007 to March 2009 and non-U.S. equity markets fell more than 60 percent. As of this writing (May 2011), stocks worldwide have made a strong recovery and are now within 15 percent of their all-time highs.

Nevertheless, the returns for stocks during the past decade have not been good. Since the first forum was held, the stock returns on the broad-based Russell 3000 Index have averaged 5.6 percent per year; when offset against 2.5 percent annual inflation, the real return is only a little more than 3 percent per year. The nominal yields on Treasuries have averaged 2.2 percent during the decade, leaving a real return of −0.2 percent per year on those instruments. These returns mean that the realized equity premium, or excess return of stocks over T-bills, has been between 3 percent and 3.5 percent. These numbers are not far from the predictions that I made at the first forum 10 years ago. At the time, I expected real returns of equities to be 4.5–5.5 percent and an equity risk premium of 2 percent (200 bps).

As I read through my analysis from 10 years ago, I could see that the main reason I overestimated the real return on stocks was that I overestimated the price-to-earnings ratio (P/E) that investors would pay for stocks. There were good reasons back then for why the P/E of stocks should be higher than its historical average of 15, a level computed from earnings data extending back to 1871, and should instead range between 20 and 25. First, the sharp decline in transaction costs caused by the development of index funds and the plunge in commission prices gave investors a much more favorable realized risk–return trade-off than they received in earlier years. Another reason I conjectured that the P/E would be higher than its historical level was the decline in the volatility of real economy variables. This increase in macroeconomic stability was termed by economists at the time as the "Great Moderation."

Of course, the 2007–09 recession dispelled the idea that the business cycle had been tamed. It is my opinion that the Great Moderation was indeed real, but the long period of macroeconomic stability led to an excessive decline in risk premiums, particularly in housing-related securities. So, when real estate prices unexpectedly fell, the entire financial system came crashing down. The financial crisis greatly increased the risk aversion of investors, and that result brought the P/E back down to historical levels and led to the poor stock returns of the past decade.

This observation can be confirmed by examining the data. When the first forum was held in November 2001, the reported earnings of the S&P 500 over the preceding 12 months were $15.90, which yielded a P/E of 36.77. The trailing 12-month earnings on the S&P 500 at the time of the second forum in January 2011 were $81.47, more than a threefold increase. Yet the index itself was up by only 30 percent, and the P/E had fallen to 16.66. If the P/E had fallen only to 22.5, the middle of my valuation range, stock returns would have been about 3 percentage points per year higher.

Another prediction that did not materialize was my estimate of future bond yields. I believed that the real yields on bonds would remain between 3 and 4 percent, the level that prevailed when Treasury Inflation-Protected Securities (TIPS) were first issued in 1997. I also believed that the realized bond returns in the period after World War II (WWII) were biased downward because of the unanticipated inflation from the late 1960s through the early 1980s. So, I did not consider historical returns on bonds; instead, I used the current yield on TIPS in making my forecast for future bond yields.

Instead, real yields fell dramatically, especially in the wake of the financial crisis. As of early 2011, 10-year TIPS yields are less than 1 percent and 5-year TIPS yields are negative. The two primary reasons for the drop in real yields are the slowdown in economic growth and the increase in the risk aversion of the investing public, which, in turn, is caused by both the aging of the population and the shocks associated with the financial crisis. The decline in inflation has caused the yields on nominal bonds to drop even more, generating very large realized returns for nominal bond investors. Over the last decade, realized bond returns were 4.7 percent per year after inflation, swamping stock returns. Over the past 20 years, realized bond returns were 6.0 percent per year, 1 percentage point less than the 7.0 percent real returns on stocks.

Updated Return Data

Table 1 shows historical returns for stocks, bonds, and T-bills from 1802 through April 2011. The past decade has shaved one-tenth of a percent off of the annualized real returns on stocks from 1802 through April 2001; three-tenths off of the equity returns from 1871, which is when the Cowles Foundation for Research in Economics data became available; and five-tenths off of the real return since 1926, which is the period that Ibbotson and Sinquefield popularized in their research.[1] Over all long-term periods, the real return on stocks remained in the 6–7 percent range. Over the past 30 years, the real annual return on stocks has been 7.9 percent, and over the past 20 years, the real return has been 7.0 percent. In fact, the numbers that now fill the table are almost identical to those that I calculated when I started my research in the late 1980s. In essence, the poor returns of the past 10 years just offset the very high returns of the previous decade.

Table 2 summarizes some of the important statistics about the equity market, such as the P/E, earnings growth, and dividend growth, for 1871–April 2011. The average P/E has changed very little over the past decade. In the version of Table 2 prepared for the 2001 forum, the average P/E was 14.45; adding the subsequent 10 years of data increased it by 0.06 to 14.51. The earnings yield, which is the reciprocal of the P/E, obviously also changes little.

One important issue that was in contention in the first forum is still debated today. Finance theory, particularly that of Modigliani and Miller (M&M), predicts that when the dividend payout ratio declines, the dividend yield will also decline, but this decline will be offset by an increase in the growth rate of future earnings and dividends.[2] Cliff Asness, at the 2001 forum, and Rob Arnott, at the most recent forum, cite research, which they performed together, that suggests that a lower payout ratio, in contrast to what finance theory would predict, does not actually lead to faster earnings growth.[3] At the first forum, I claimed that this finding was a result of the cyclical behavior of earnings. Asness and Arnott claimed to have run further tests to contest this point. Notwithstanding their results, my data clearly show that over long periods of time, the payout ratio is inversely correlated with dividend and earnings growth as predicted by finance theory.

---

[1] Roger G. Ibbotson and Rex A. Sinquefield, "Stocks, Bonds, Bills, and Inflation: Year-by-Year Historical Returns (1926–1974)," *Journal of Business*, vol. 49, no. 1 (January 1976):11–47.

[2] Franco Modigliani and Merton H. Miller, "The Cost of Capital, Corporation Finance and the Theory of Investment," *American Economic Review*, vol. 48, no. 3 (June 1958):261–297.

[3] Robert D. Arnott and Clifford S. Asness, "Surprise! Higher Dividends = Higher Earnings Growth," *Financial Analysts Journal*, vol. 59, no. 1 (January/February 2003):70–87.

Table 1. Historical Returns for Stocks, Bonds, and T-Bills, 1802–April 2011

| | Real Return | | | | | | Stocks' Excess Return Over | | | |
| | Stocks | | Bonds | | T-Bills | | Bonds | | T-Bills | |
	Geometric	Arithmetic	Geometric	Arithmetic	Geometric	Arithmetic	Geometric	Arithmetic	Geometric	Arithmetic
Periods										
1802–2011	6.7%	8.2%	3.6%	3.9%	2.7%	2.9%	3.1%	4.3%	3.9%	5.3%
1870–2011	6.5	8.2	3.0	3.3	1.6	1.7	3.5	4.9	4.9	6.5
Major subperiods										
1802–1870	7.0	8.3	4.8	5.1	5.1	5.4	2.2	3.2	1.9	2.9
1871–1925	6.6	7.9	3.7	3.9	3.2	3.3	2.9	4.0	3.5	4.7
1926–2011	6.4	8.4	2.5	3.0	0.6	0.7	4.0	5.4	5.8	7.7
After World War II										
1946–2011	6.4%	8.3%	1.8%	2.2%	0.5%	0.6%	4.6%	6.0%	6.0%	7.6%
1946–1965	10.0	11.4	-1.2	-1.0	-0.8	-0.7	11.2	12.3	10.9	12.1
1966–1981	-0.4	1.4	-4.2	-3.9	-0.2	-0.1	3.8	5.2	-0.2	1.5
1982–1999	13.6	14.3	8.5	9.3	2.9	2.9	5.1	5.0	10.7	11.4
1982–2011	7.9	9.1	7.5	7.9	1.8	1.7	0.4	1.2	6.1	7.4
1991–2011	7.0	8.5	6.0	6.3	0.9	0.9	0.9	2.1	6.1	7.6
2001–2011	0.8	2.8	4.7	4.7	-0.3	-0.3	-4.0	-1.9	1.1	3.0

Table 2. Historical Equity Market Statistics, 1871–April 2011

	Real Stock Return	Average P/E	Inverse of Average P/E	Real Earnings Growth	Real Dividend Growth	Dividend Yield	Real Capital Gains	Average Payout Ratio
1871–2011	6.51%	14.51	6.89%	1.81%	1.22%	4.47%	1.55%	59.92%
1871–1945	6.39	13.83	7.23	0.67	0.74	5.31	1.11	70.81
1946–2011	6.44	15.29	6.54	3.14	1.76	3.50	2.85	47.42

In fact, the evidence in favor of M&M has been strengthened by the addition of the past 10 years of data. In the 1871–1945 data, annual real per share earnings growth was only 0.67 percent per year and the payout ratio averaged nearly 72 percent. In the post-WWII period, real earnings growth was 3.14 percent and the payout ratio was only 47.42 percent.[4]

It is true that adding the past 10 years increases post-WWII real per share dividend growth only marginally because the payout ratio is still declining and has not yet reached a new "steady state" in which dividend growth will increase to the level of earnings growth.

Projections for the Next Decade

I hope a third forum will be held in 2021 so we can look back on our predictions in 2011, either nursing our wounds or congratulating ourselves on our astuteness. Using the current P/E as a basis, I expect real stock returns to be between 6 and 7 percent. But I will not be surprised if they are higher because the same factors that influenced my prediction of P/Es in the range of 20–25 are as operative in 2011 as they were at the time of the first forum in 2001.

Real bond returns are on track to be much lower. Ten-year TIPS are now yielding about 1 percent, so the excess returns of stocks over bonds should be in the 5–6 percent range, which is higher than the historical average. And the bias, if any, will be toward a higher equity premium if real bond yields rise from their extremely low levels, as I think they should. In short, relative to bonds, stocks look extraordinarily attractive, and I expect stock investors will look back a decade from now with satisfaction.

---

[4]Note that the 3.14 percent growth rate is more than 1 percentage point higher than the post-WWII real earnings growth rate presented at the first forum; the addition of the past 10 years also reduces the post-WWII average payout ratio from 50.75 percent to 47.42 percent.

The Equity Premium Puzzle Revisited

Rajnish Mehra

E.N. Basha Arizona Heritage Chair Professor of Finance and Economics, Arizona State University
Research Associate, NBER

In the two and a half decades since "The Equity Premium: A Puzzle" (Mehra and Prescott 1985) was published, attempts to successfully account for the equity premium have become a major research impetus in finance and economics. In an effort to reconcile theory with observations, I will elaborate on the appropriateness of three crucial abstractions in that article. In particular, I will argue that our finding (i.e., the premium for bearing nondiversifiable aggregate risk is small) is not inconsistent with the average equity premium over the past 120 years.

The three abstractions that I address here are

- using T-bill prices as a proxy for the expected intertemporal marginal rate of substitution of consumption;

- ignoring the difference between borrowing and lending rates (a consequence of agent heterogeneity and costly intermediation);

- abstracting from life-cycle effects and borrowing constraints on the young.

I examine each of these in detail below.

Using T-Bill Prices as a Proxy for the Expected Intertemporal Marginal Rate of Substitution of Consumption

An assumption implicit in Mehra and Prescott (1985) is that agents use both equity and the riskless asset to smooth consumption intertemporally. This assumption is a direct consequence of the first-order condition (see Equation 1) for the representative household in our model. It implies that agents save by optimally allocating resources between equity and riskless debt.

$$0 = E_t \left[\frac{U_c(c_{t+s})}{U_c(c_t)} \left(r^e_{t,t+s} - r^d_{t,t+s} \right) \right]. \tag{1}$$

Author Note: This paper draws widely on my collaborations with George Constantinides, John Donaldson, and Edward Prescott. Quite independently of our joint work, they have made substantial contributions to the literature on the equity premium puzzle. Consequently, the views expressed in this paper do not necessarily reflect their views.

Equation 1 is the standard asset-pricing equation in macroeconomics and finance. $U_c(c_{t+s})$ is the marginal utility of consumption at time $t + s$; $re_{t,t+s}$ and $rd_{t,t+s}$ are, respectively, the return on equity and the return on the riskless asset over the period t, $t + s$; and E_t is the expectation conditional on the agent's information set at time t.

If the results from the model are to be compared with data, it is crucial to identify the empirical counterpart of the riskless asset that is actually used by agents to smooth consumption. In Mehra and Prescott (1985), we used the highly liquid T-bill rate, corrected for expected inflation, as a proxy for this asset. But one might ask: Is it reasonable to assume that T-bills are an appropriate proxy for the riskless asset that agents use to save for retirement and smooth consumption? Do households actually hold T-bills to finance their retirement? *Only if this question is empirically verified would it be reasonable to equate their expected marginal rate of substitution of consumption to the rate of return on T-bills.*

This question cannot be answered in the abstract without reference to the asset holdings of households, so a natural next step is to examine the assets held by households. **Table 1** details these holdings for U.S. households. The four big asset-holding categories of households are tangible assets, pension and life insurance holdings, equity (both corporate and noncorporate), and debt assets.

Table 1. Household Assets and Liabilities as a Fraction/ Multiple of GDP
(average of 2000 and 2005)

Assets (GDP)		Liabilities (GDP)	
Asset	GDP (×)	Liability	GDP (×)
Tangible household	1.65	Liabilities	0.7
Corporate equity	0.85	Net worth	4.15
Noncorporate equity	0.5		
Pension and life insurance reserves	1.0		
Debt assets	0.85		
Total	4.85		4.85

In 2000, privately held government debt was only 0.30 times GDP, a third of which was held by foreigners. The amount of interest-bearing government debt with maturity less than a year was only 0.085 times GDP, which is a small fraction of total household net worth. Virtually no T-bills are directly owned by households.[1] Approximately one-third of the T-bills outstanding are held by foreign central banks, and two-thirds are held by U.S. financial institutions.

---

[1]See Table B-89, *Economic Report of the President* (2005).

Although large amounts of debt assets are held, most of these are in pension fund and life insurance reserves. Some are in demand deposits, for which free services are provided. Most government debt is held indirectly; a small fraction is held as savings bonds.

Thus, much of intertemporal saving is in debt assets, such as annuities and mortgage debt, held in retirement accounts and as pension fund reserves. Other assets, not T-bills, are typically held to finance consumption in retirement. *Hence, T-bills and short-term debt are not reasonable empirical counterparts to the risk-free asset priced in Equation 1,* and it would be inappropriate to equate the return on these assets to the expected marginal rate of substitution for an important group of agents.

An inflation-indexed, default-free bond portfolio with a duration similar to that of a well-diversified equity portfolio would be a reasonable proxy for a risk-free asset used for consumption smoothing.[2] For most of the 20th century, equity has had an implied duration of about 25 years, so a portfolio of TIPS (Treasury Inflation-Protected Securities) of a similar duration would be a reasonable proxy.

Because TIPS have only recently (1997) been introduced in U.S. capital markets, it is difficult to get accurate estimates of the mean return on this asset class. The average return for the 1997–2005 period is 3.7 percent. An alternative (though imperfect) proxy would be to use the returns on indexed mortgages guaranteed by Ginnie Mae (Government National Mortgage Association) or issued by Fannie Mae (Federal National Mortgage Association). I conjecture that if these indexed default-free securities are used as a benchmark, the equity premium will be closer to 4 percent than to the 6 percent equity premium relative to T-bills. By using a more appropriate benchmark for the riskless asset, I can account for 2 percentage points of the "equity premium."

Ignoring the Difference between Borrowing and Lending Rates

A major disadvantage of the homogeneous household construct is that it precludes the modeling of borrowing and lending among agents. In equilibrium, the shadow price of consumption at date $t + 1$ in terms of consumption at date t is such that the amount of borrowing and lending is zero. However, there is a large amount of costly intermediated borrowing and lending between households, and as a consequence, borrowing rates exceed lending rates. When borrowing and lending rates differ, a question arises: Should the equity premium be measured relative to the riskless borrowing rate or the riskless lending rate?

---

[2]McGrattan and Prescott (2003) use long-term high-grade municipal bonds as a proxy for the riskless security.

To address this question, Mehra, Piguillem, and Prescott (2011) constructed a model that incorporates agent heterogeneity and costly financial intermediation. The resources used in intermediation (3.4 percent of GNP) and the amount intermediated (1.7 percent of GNP) imply that the average household borrowing rate is at least 2 percentage points higher than the average household lending rate. Relative to the level of the observed average rates of return on debt and equity securities, this spread is far from being insignificant and cannot be ignored when addressing the equity premium.

In this model,[3] a subset of households both borrow money and hold equity. Consequently, a no-arbitrage condition is that the return on equity and the borrowing rate are equal (5 percent). The return on government debt, the household lending rate, is 3 percent. If I use the conventional definition of the equity premium—the return on a broad equity index less the return on government debt—I would erroneously conclude that in this model, the equity premium is 2 percent. The difference between the government borrowing rate and the return on equity is not an equity premium; it arises because of the wedge between borrowing and lending rates. Analogously, if borrowing and lending rates for equity investors differ, and they do in the U.S. economy, the equity premium should be measured relative to the investor borrowing rate rather than the investor lending rate (the government's borrowing rate). Measuring the premium relative to the government's borrowing rate artificially increases the premium for bearing aggregate risk by the difference between the investor's borrowing and lending rates.[4] If such a correction is made to the benchmark discussed earlier, the "equity premium" is further reduced by 2 percentage points. Thus, I have accounted for 4 percentage points of the equity premium reported in Mehra and Prescott (1985) by factors other than aggregate risk.

Abstracting from Life-Cycle Effects and Borrowing Constraints on the Young

In Constantinides, Donaldson, and Mehra (2002), we examined the impact of life-cycle effects, such as variable labor income and borrowing constraints, on the equity premium. We illustrated these ideas in an overlapping-generations exchange economy in which consumers live for three periods. In the first period, a period of human capital acquisition, the consumer receives a relatively low endowment income. In the second period, the consumer is employed and receives wage income subject to large uncertainty. In the third period, the consumer retires and consumes the assets accumulated in the second period.

---

[3]There is no aggregate uncertainty in our model.

[4]For a detailed exposition of this and related issues, see Mehra and Prescott (2008).

In the article, we explored the implications of a borrowing constraint by deriving and contrasting the stationary equilibriums in two versions of the economy. In the *borrowing-constrained* version, the young are prohibited from borrowing and from selling equity short. The *borrowing-unconstrained* economy differs from the borrowing-constrained one only in that the borrowing constraint and the short-sale constraint are absent.

The attractiveness of equity as an asset depends on the correlation between consumption and equity income. Because the marginal utility of consumption varies inversely with consumption, equity will command a higher price (and consequently, a lower rate of return) if it pays off in states when consumption is high and vice versa.[5]

A key insight of ours in the article is that as the correlation of equity income with consumption changes over the life cycle of an individual, so does the attractiveness of equity as an asset. Consumption can be decomposed into the sum of wages and equity income. Young people looking forward at the start of their lives have uncertain future wage and equity income; furthermore, the correlation of equity income with consumption will not be particularly high as long as stock and wage income are not highly correlated. This is empirically the case, as documented by Davis and Willen (2000). Equity will, therefore, be a hedge against fluctuations in wages and a "desirable" asset to hold as far as the young are concerned.

The same asset (equity) has a very different characteristic for the middle-aged. Their wage uncertainty has largely been resolved. Their future retirement wage income is either zero or deterministic, and the innovations (fluctuations) in their consumption occur from fluctuations in equity income. At this stage of the life cycle, equity income is highly correlated with consumption. Consumption is high when equity income is high, and equity is no longer a hedge against fluctuations in consumption; hence, for this group, equity requires a higher rate of return.

The characteristics of equity as an asset, therefore, change depending on the predominant holder of the equity. Life-cycle considerations thus become crucial for asset pricing. If equity is a desirable asset for the marginal investor in the economy, then the observed equity premium will be low relative to an economy where the marginal investor finds it unattractive to hold equity. The *deus ex machina* is the stage in the life cycle of the marginal investor.

---

[5]This is precisely the reason why high-beta stocks in the simple capital asset pricing model framework have a high rate of return. In that model, the return on the market is a proxy for consumption. High-beta stocks pay off when the market return is high—that is, when marginal utility is low and, hence, their price is (relatively) low and their rate of return high.

We argued that the young, who should be holding equity in an economy without frictions, are effectively shut out of this market because of borrowing constraints. The young are characterized by low wages; ideally, they would like to smooth lifetime consumption by borrowing against future wage income (consuming a part of the loan and investing the rest in higher return equity). However, they are prevented from doing so because human capital alone does not collateralize major loans in modern economies for reasons of moral hazard and adverse selection.

Therefore, in the presence of borrowing constraints, equity is exclusively priced by middle-aged investors because the young are effectively excluded from the equity markets and a high equity premium is thus observed. If the borrowing constraint is relaxed, the young will borrow to purchase equity, thereby raising the bond yield. The increase in the bond yield induces the middle-aged to shift their portfolio holdings from equities to bonds. The increase in demand for equity by the young and the decrease in demand for equity by the middle-aged work in opposite directions. On balance, the effect is to increase both the equity and the bond return, while shrinking the equity premium.

The results suggest that, depending on the parameterization, between 2 and 4 percentage points of the observed equity premium can be accounted for by incorporating life-cycle effects and borrowing constraints.

Conclusion

I have argued that using an appropriate benchmark for the risk-free rate, accounting for the difference between borrowing and lending rates, and incorporating life-cycle features can account for the equity premium. That this can be accomplished without resorting to risk supports the conclusion of Mehra and Prescott (1985) that the premium for bearing systematic risk is small.

My projection for the equity premium is that at the end of the next decade, it will be higher than that observed in the past. During the next 10 years, the ratio of the retired population to the working-age population will increase. These retired households, in an attempt to hedge against outliving their assets, will likely rebalance their portfolios by substituting annuity-like products for equity. Because, in equilibrium, all assets must be held, this substitution will lead to an increase in the expected equity premium. Consequently, during this adjustment process, the realized equity premium will probably be lower than the historical average.

REFERENCES

Constantinides, G.M., J.B. Donaldson, and R. Mehra. 2002. "Junior Can't Borrow: A New Perspective on the Equity Premium Puzzle." *Quarterly Journal of Economics*, vol. 117, no. 1 (February):269–296.

Davis, Stephen J., and Paul Willen. 2000. "Using Financial Assets to Hedge Labor Income Risk: Estimating the Benefits." Working paper, University of Chicago.

McGrattan, E.R., and E.C. Prescott. 2003. "Average Debt and Equity Returns: Puzzling?" *American Economic Review*, vol. 93, no. 2 (May):392–397.

Mehra, R., and E.C. Prescott. 1985. "The Equity Premium: A Puzzle." *Journal of Monetary Economics*, vol. 15, no. 2 (March):145–161.

———. 2008. "Non-Risk-Based Explanations of the Equity Premium." In *Handbook of Investments: The Handbook of the Equity Risk Premium*. Edited by R. Mehra. Amsterdam: Elsevier.

Mehra, R., F. Piguillem, and E.C. Prescott. 2011. "Costly Financial Intermediation in Neoclassical Growth Theory." *Quantitative Economics*, vol. 2, no. 1 (March):1–36.

RESEARCH FOUNDATION CONTRIBUTION FORM

☑ **Yes,** I want the Research Foundation to continue to fund innovative research that advances the investment management profession. Please accept my tax-deductible contribution at the following level:

Contributing Research Fellow . . . .$25,000 to $49,999
Research Fellow . . . .$10,000 to $24,999
Contributing Donor . . . .$1,000 to $9,999
Donor . . . . Up to $999

I would like to donate $_____ .

☐ My check is enclosed (payable to the Research Foundation of CFA Institute).
☐ I would like to donate appreciated securities (send me information).
☐ Please charge my donation to my credit card.
  ▣ VISA   ▣ MC   ▣ Amex   ▣ Diners   ▣ Corporate   ▣ Personal

| | | | | | | | | | | | | | | | | | | |

Card Number

____ / ____
Expiration Date

Name on card   PLEASE PRINT

☐ Corporate Card
☐ Personal Card

Signature

☐ This is a pledge. Please bill me for my donation of $_____ .

☐ I would like recognition of my donation to be:
  ▣ Individual donation   ▣ Corporate donation   ▣ Different individual

PLEASE PRINT NAME OR COMPANY NAME AS YOU WOULD LIKE IT TO APPEAR

PLEASE PRINT ☐ Mr.   ☐ Mrs.   ☐ Ms.   MEMBER NUMBER_____

Last Name (Family Name)   First   Middle Initial

Title

Address

City   State/Province   Country ZIP/Postal Code

11ERP

Please mail this completed form with your contribution to:
The Research Foundation of CFA Institute • P.O. Box 2082
Charlottesville, VA 22903-0638 USA

For more on the Research Foundation of CFA Institute, please visit
www.cfainstitute.org/about/foundation/.